This Mind Map Journal Belongs To

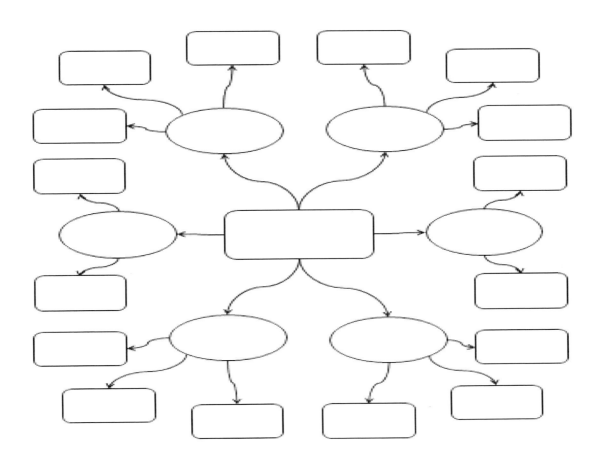

Thank you for your purchase!
If you like this notebook — Your honest Amazon rating and
review will help and will be deeply appreciated.
Thanks Again!

USING THIS MIND MAP JOURNAL

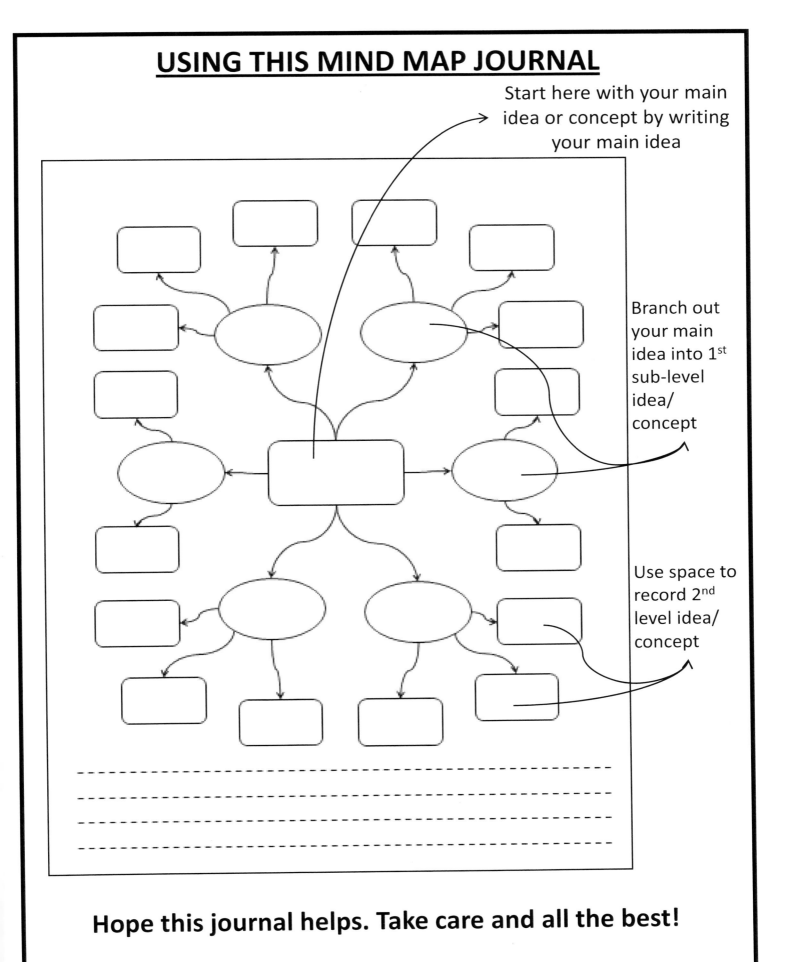

Start here with your main idea or concept by writing your main idea

Branch out your main idea into 1st sub-level idea/ concept

Use space to record 2nd level idea/ concept

Hope this journal helps. Take care and all the best!

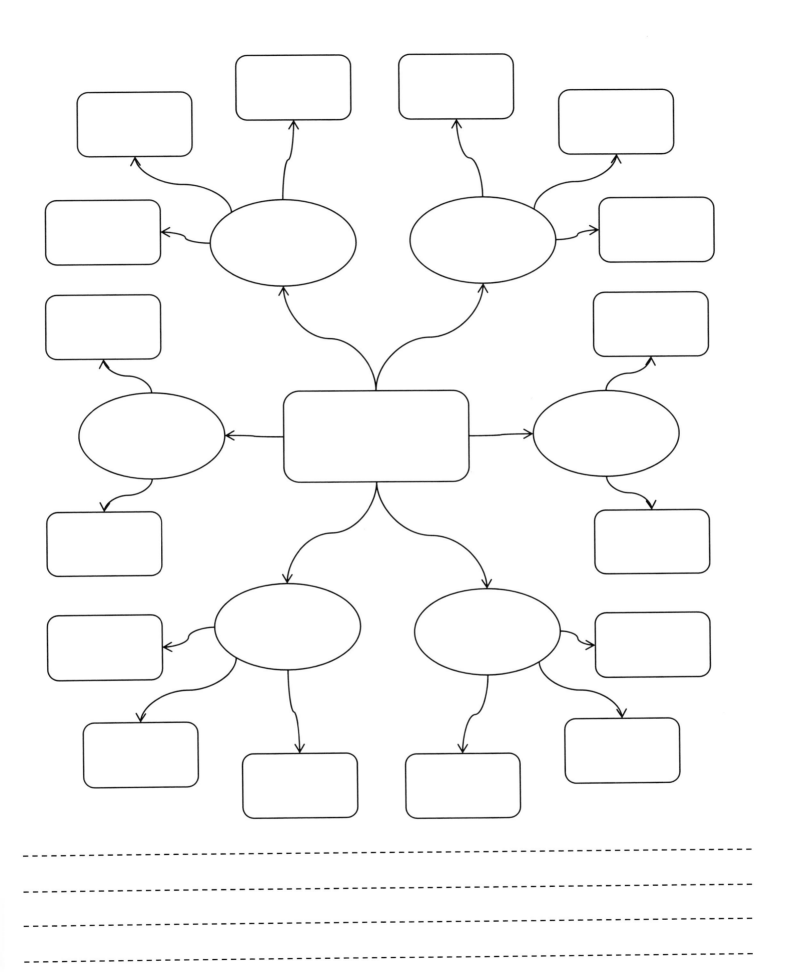

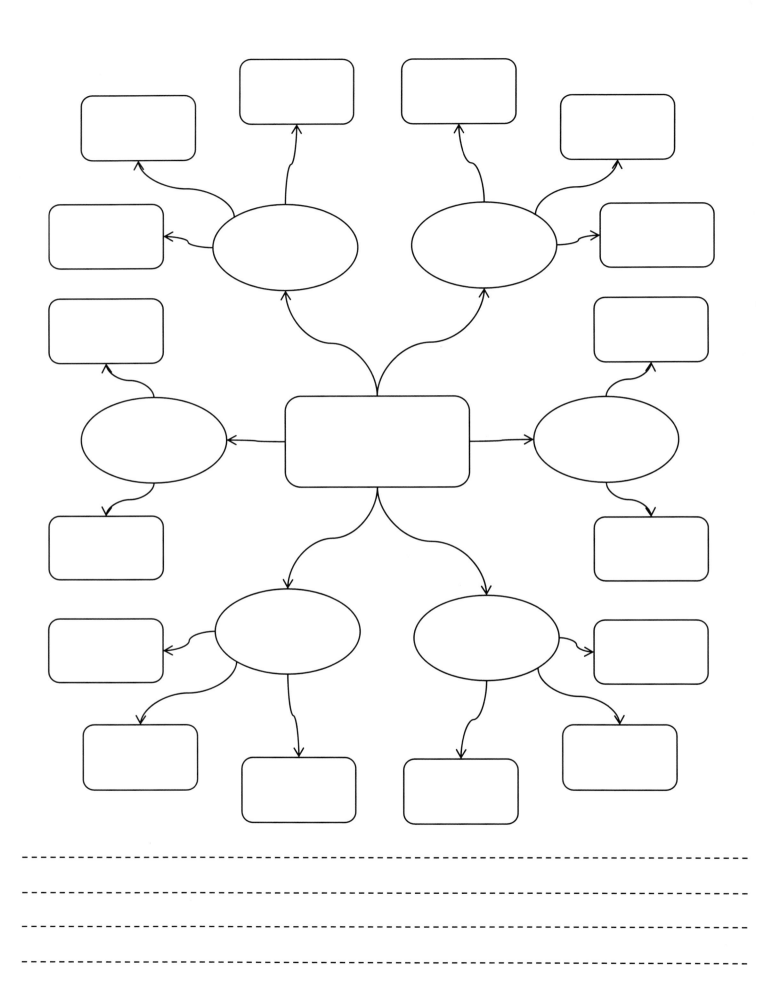

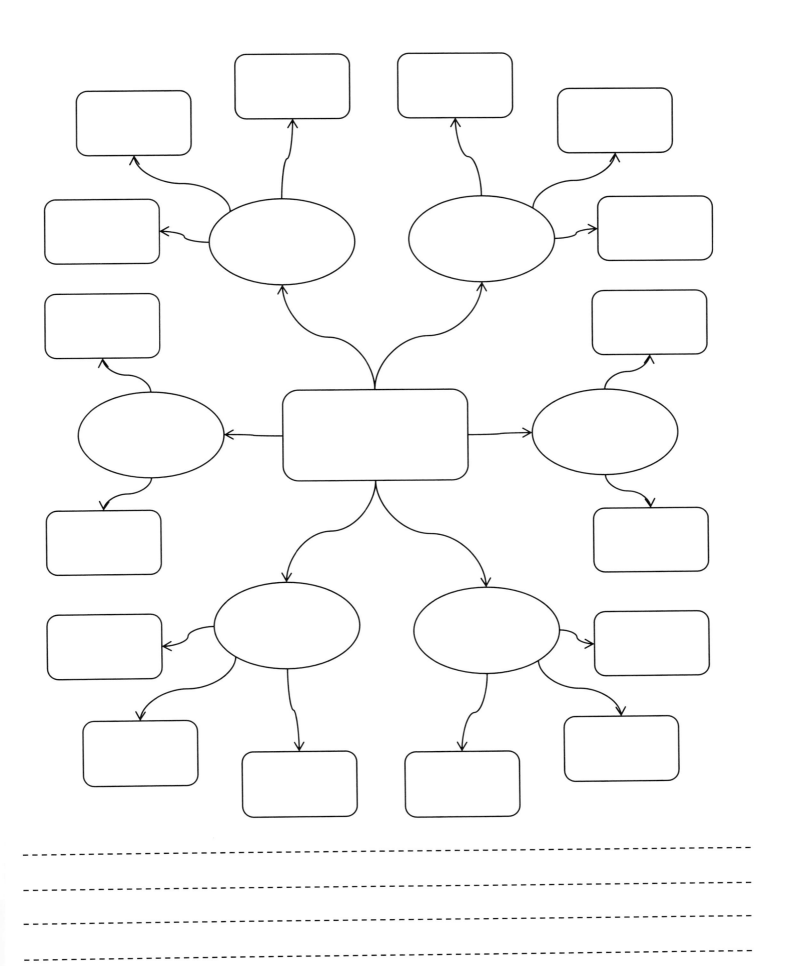

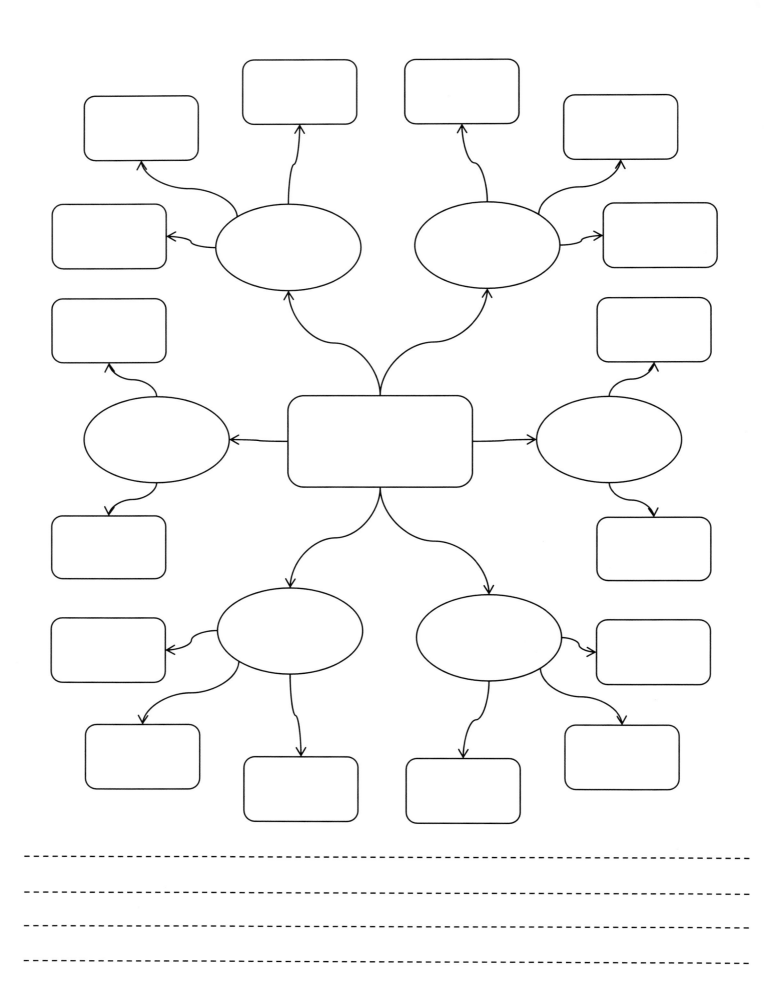

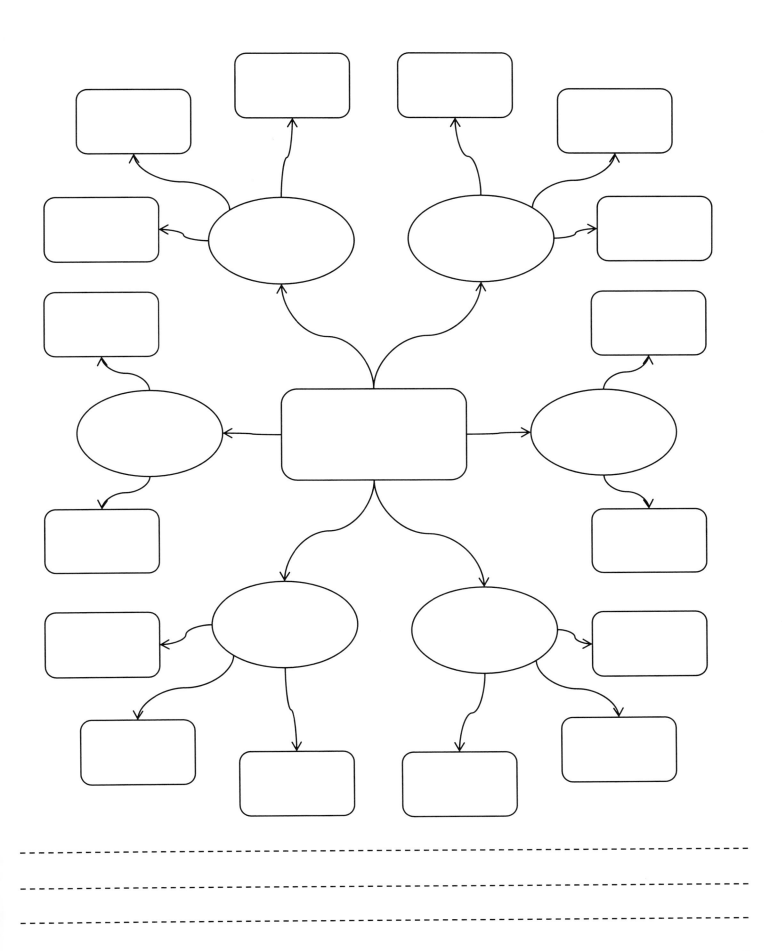

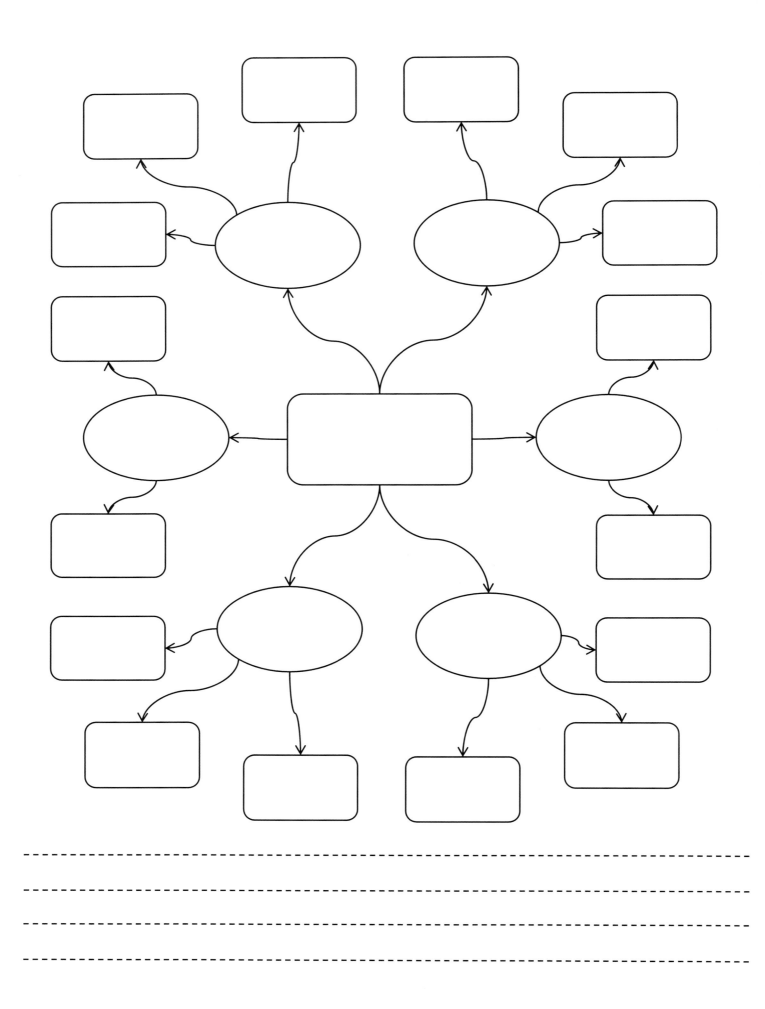

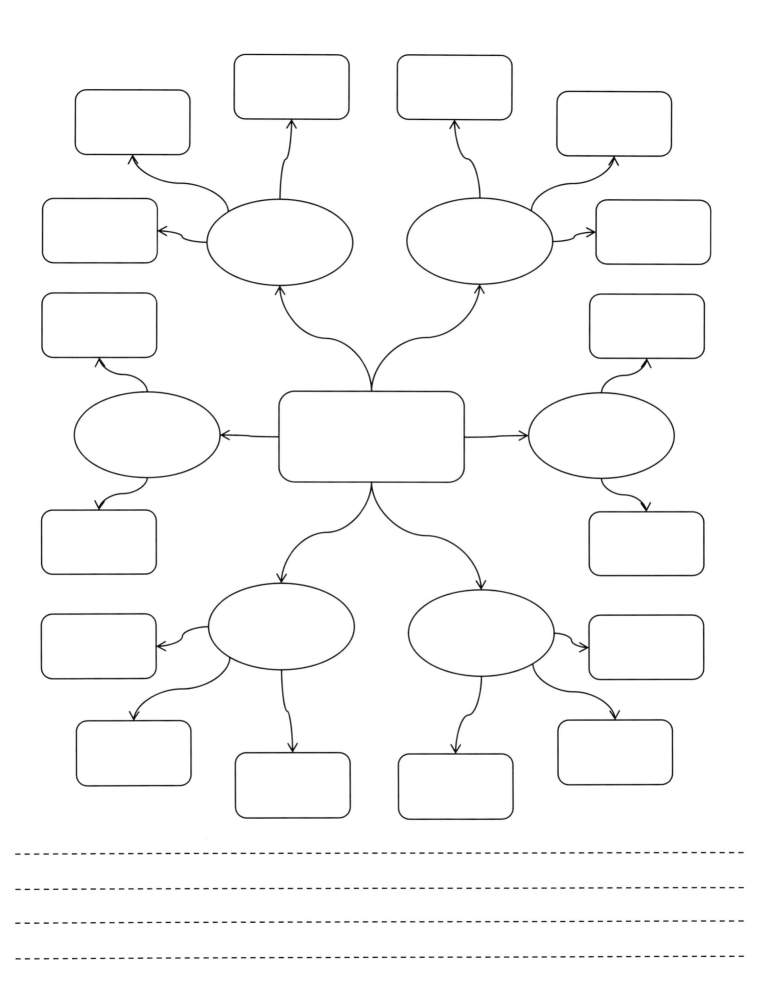

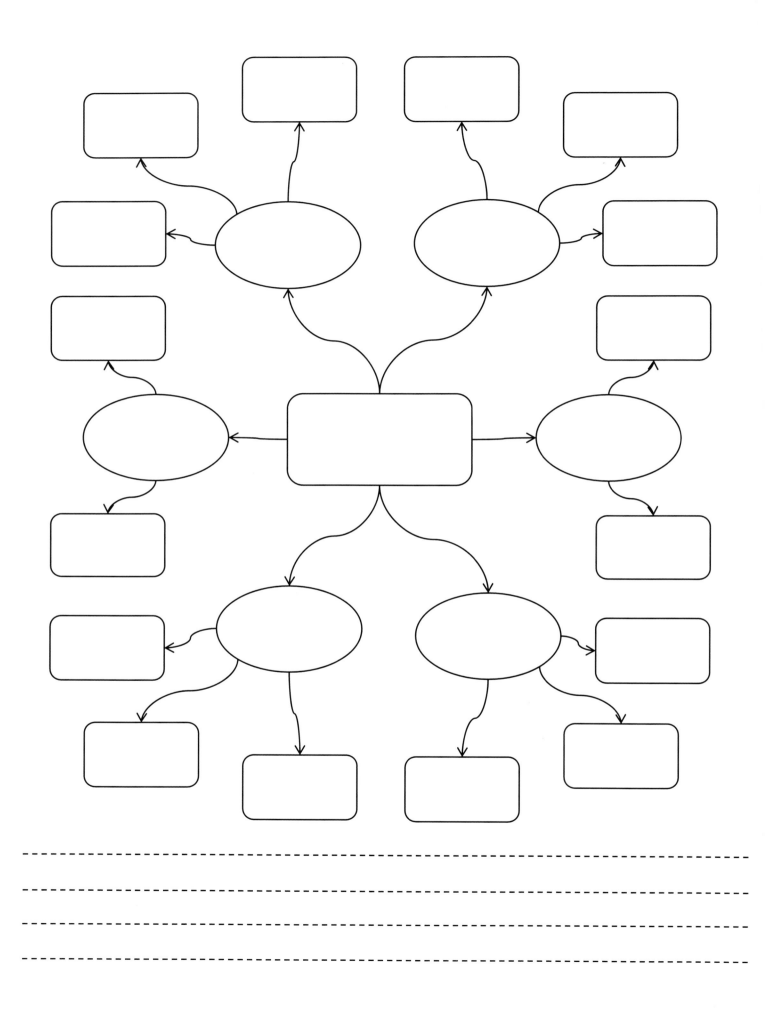

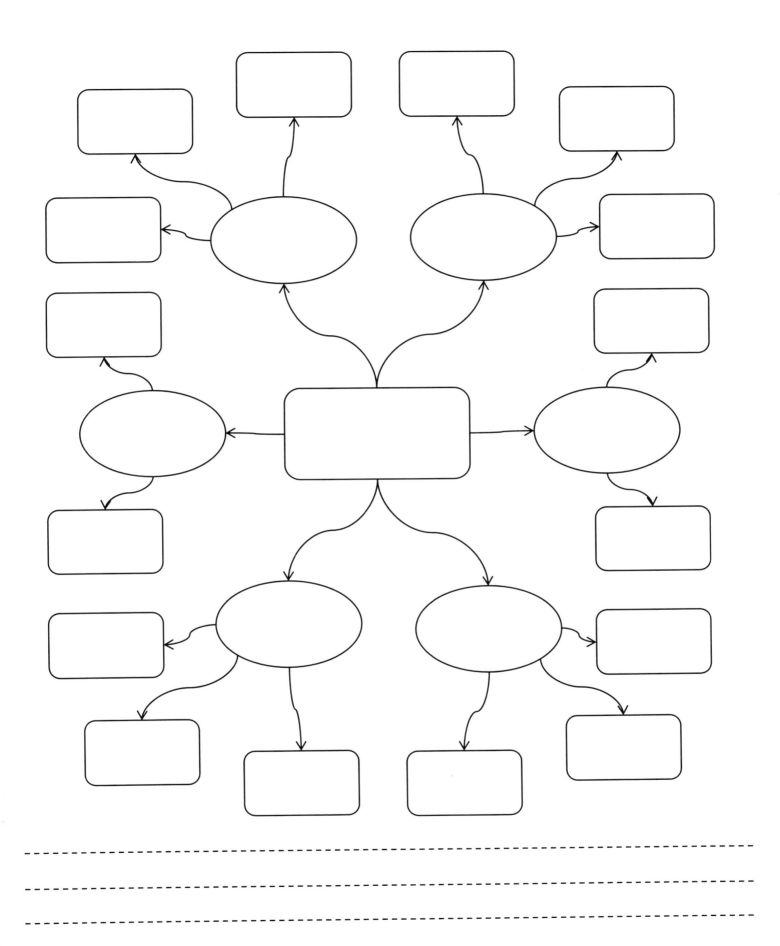

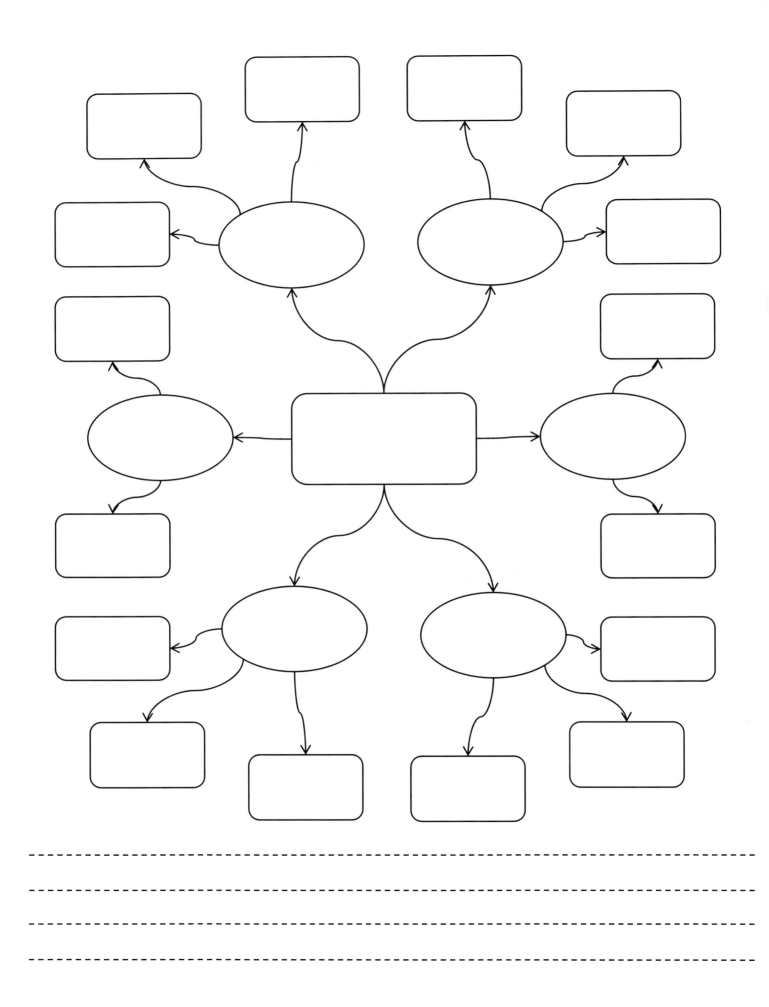

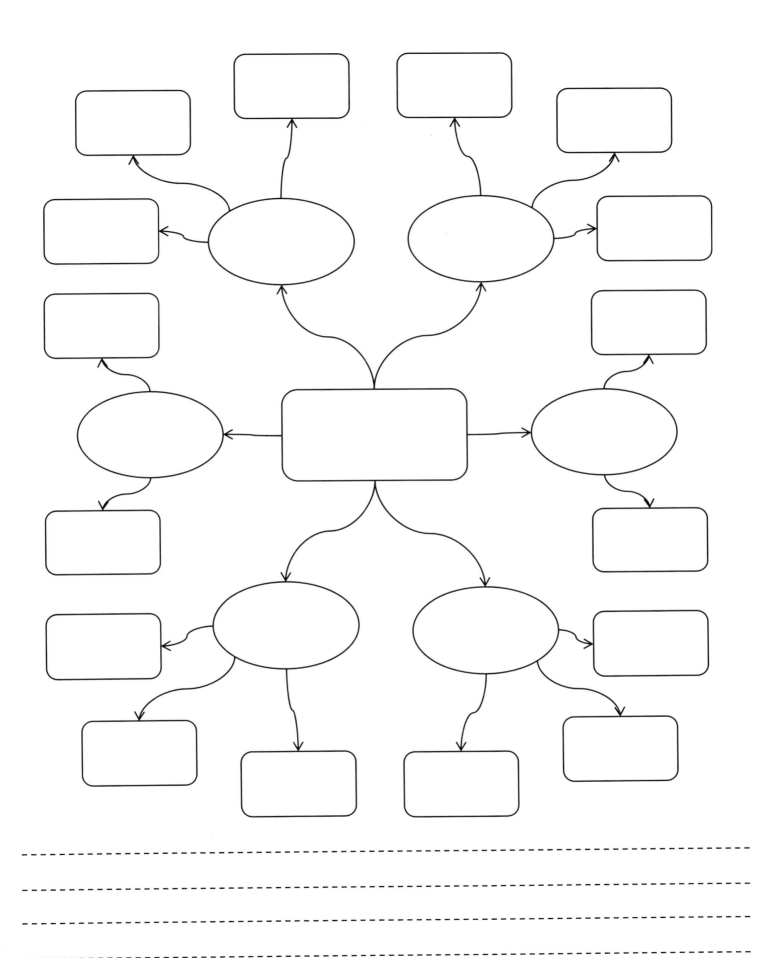

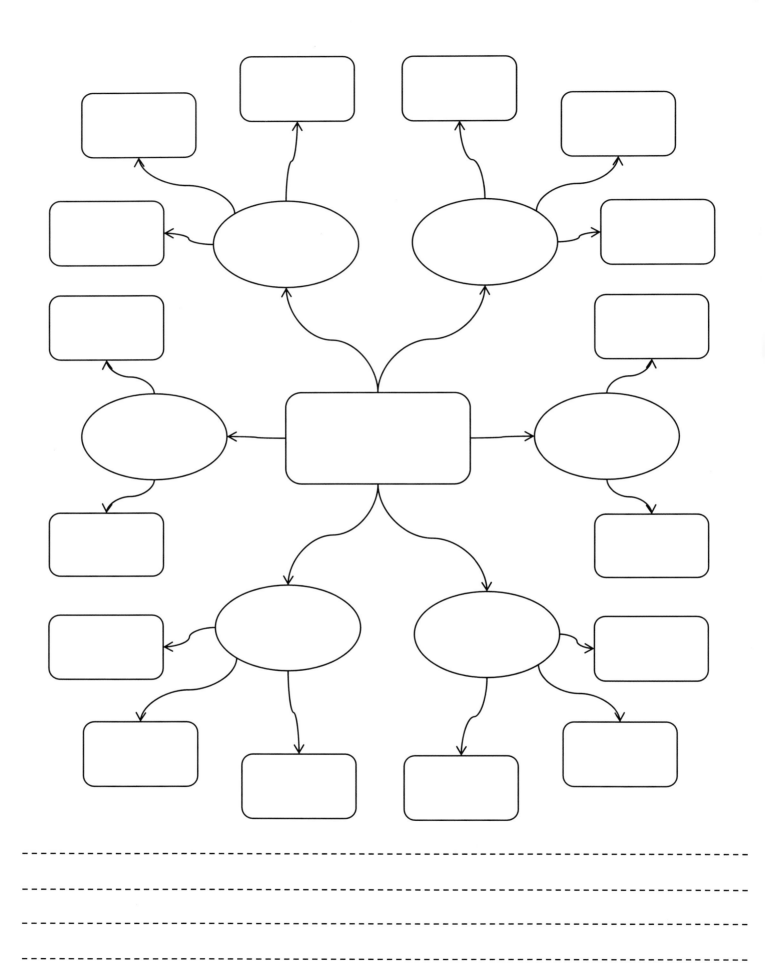

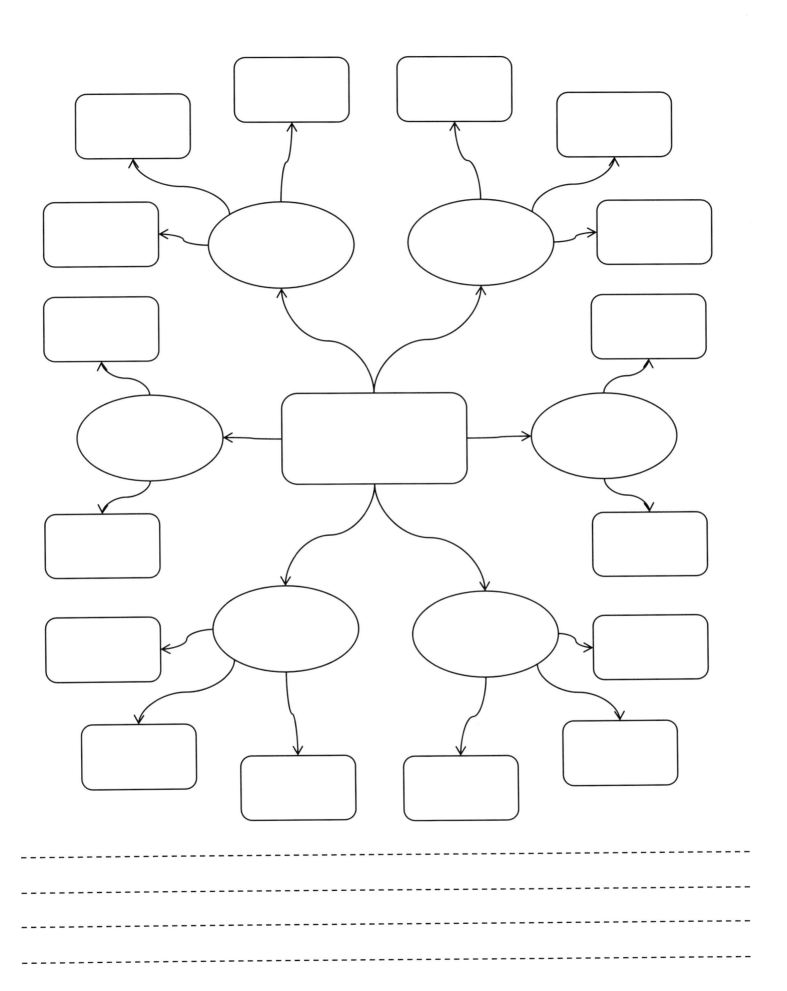

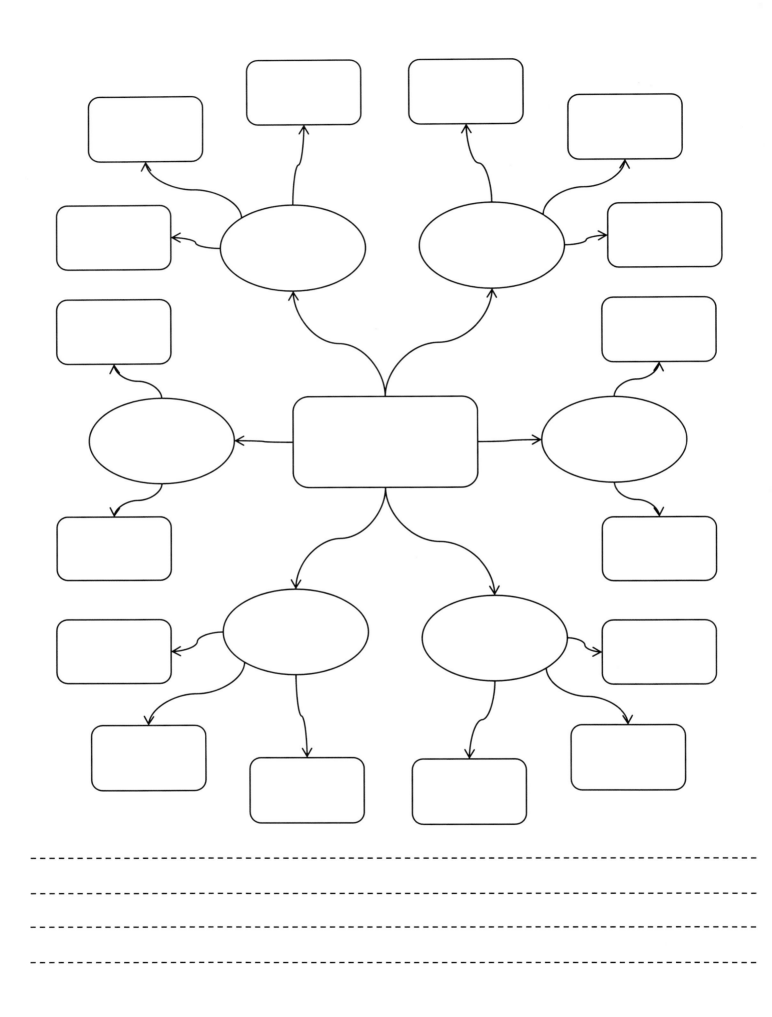

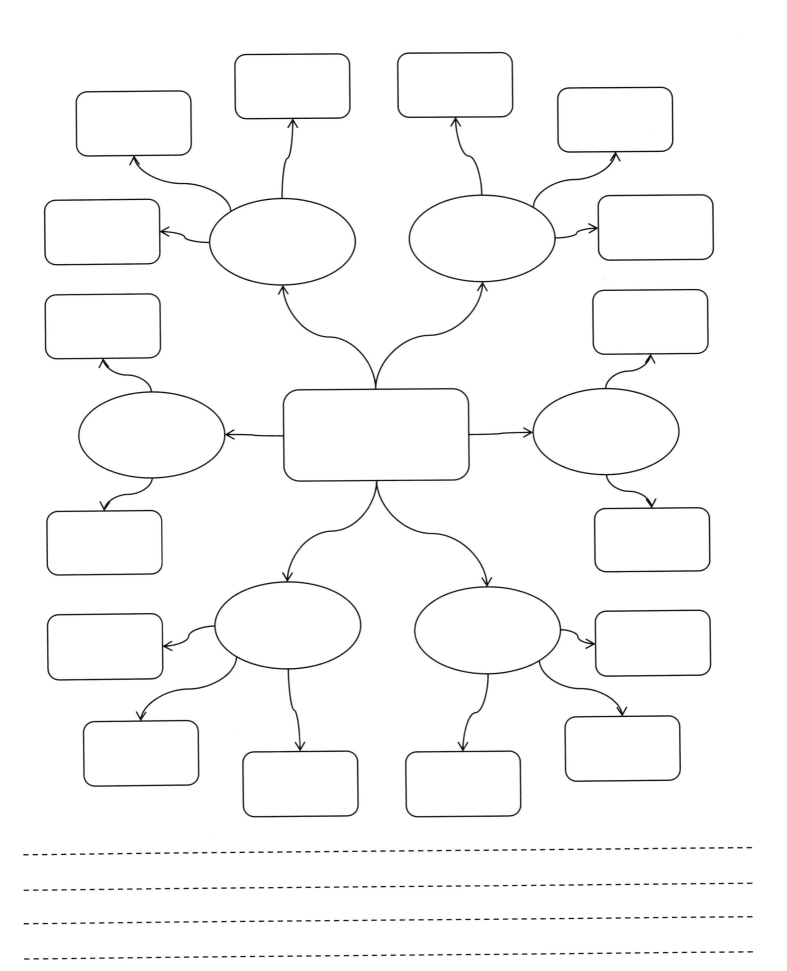

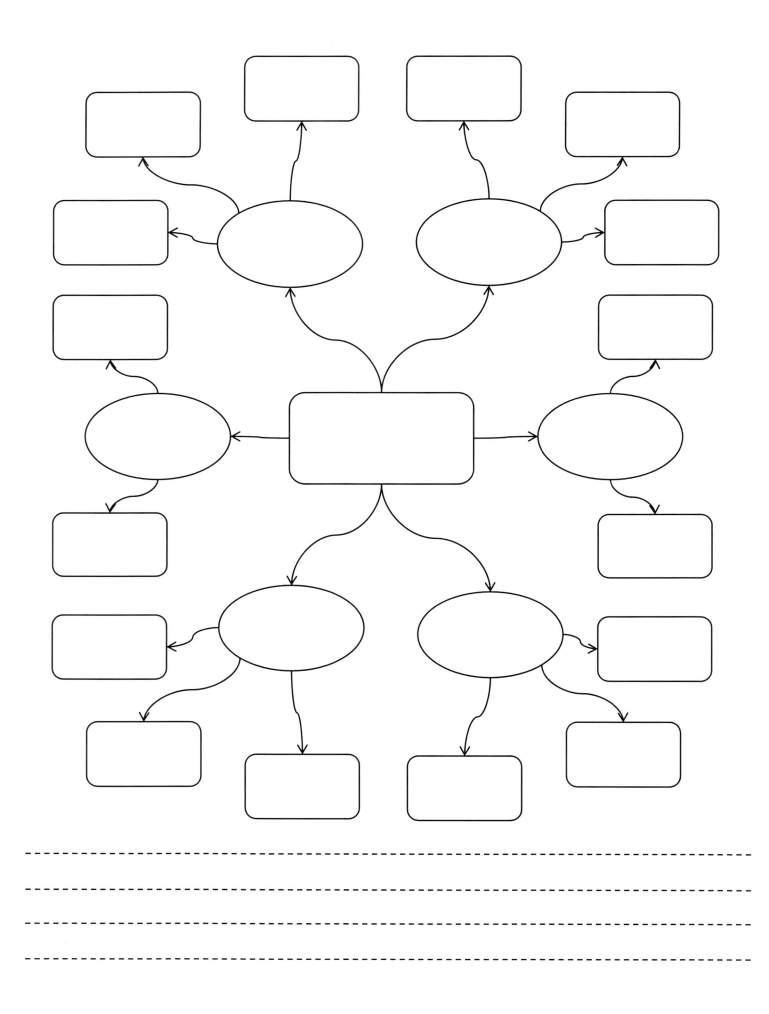

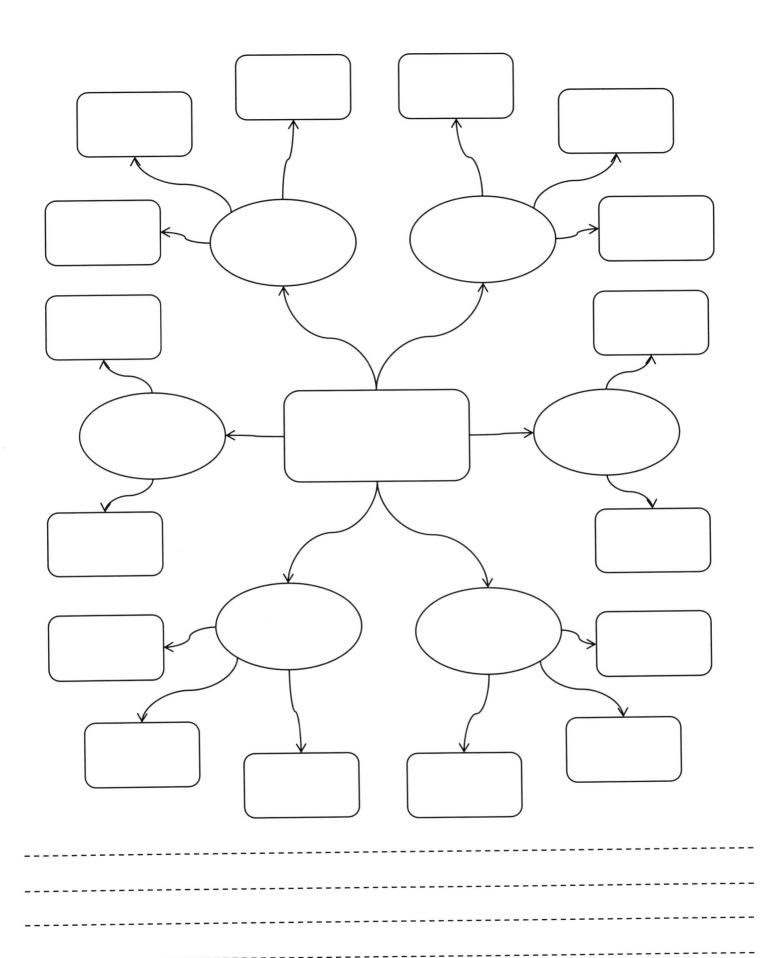

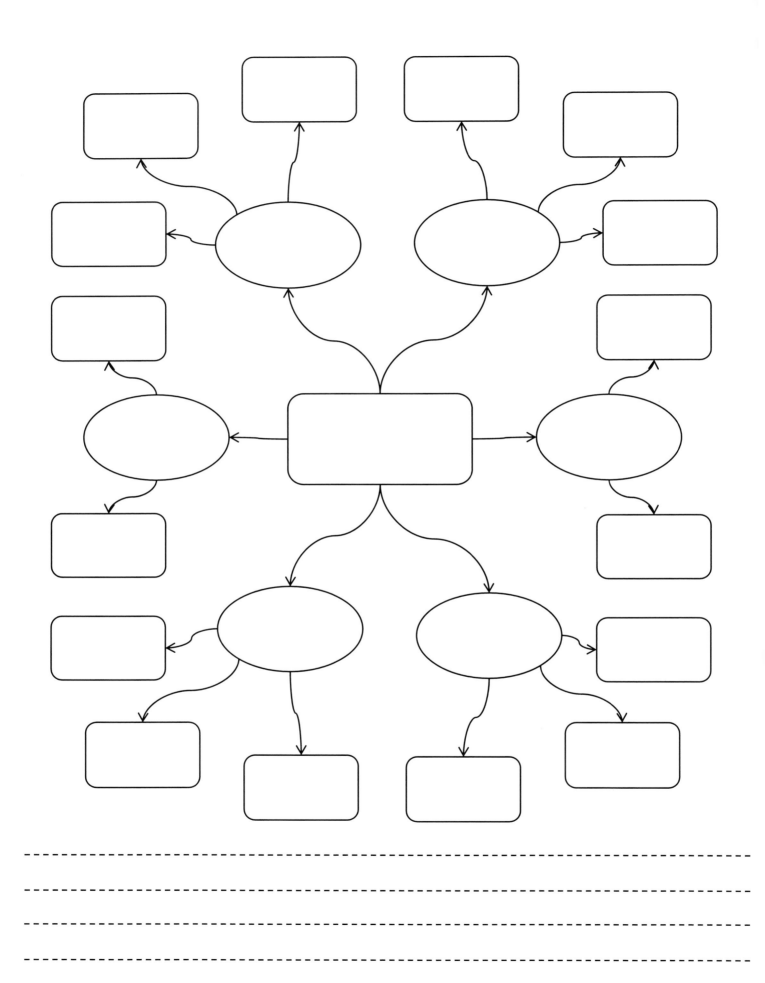

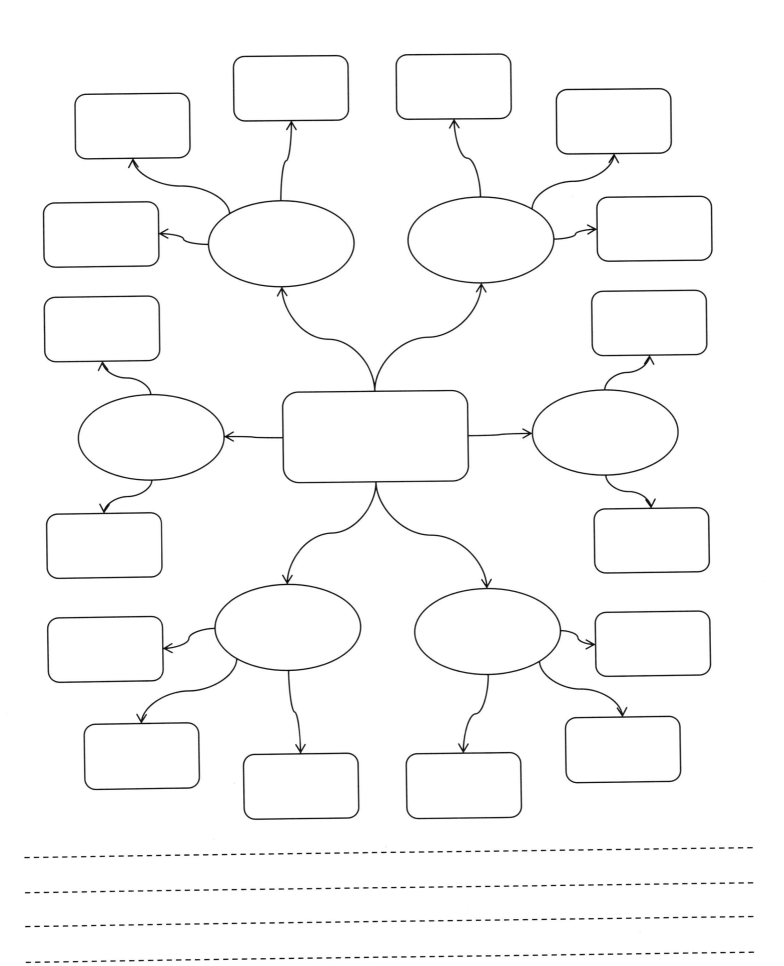

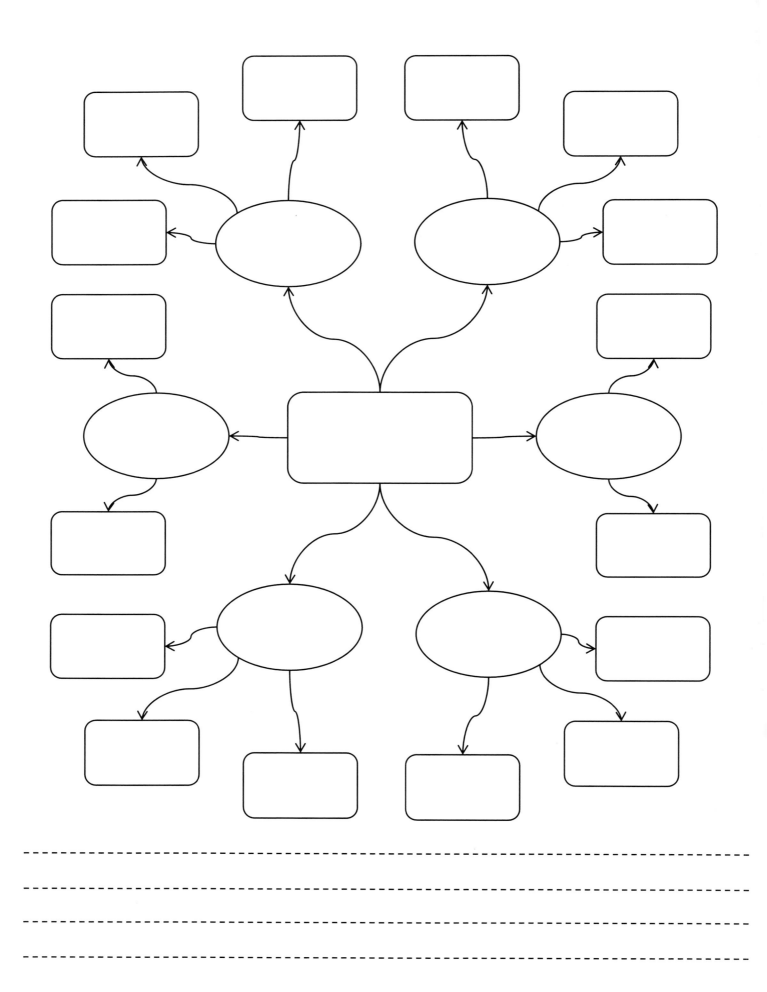

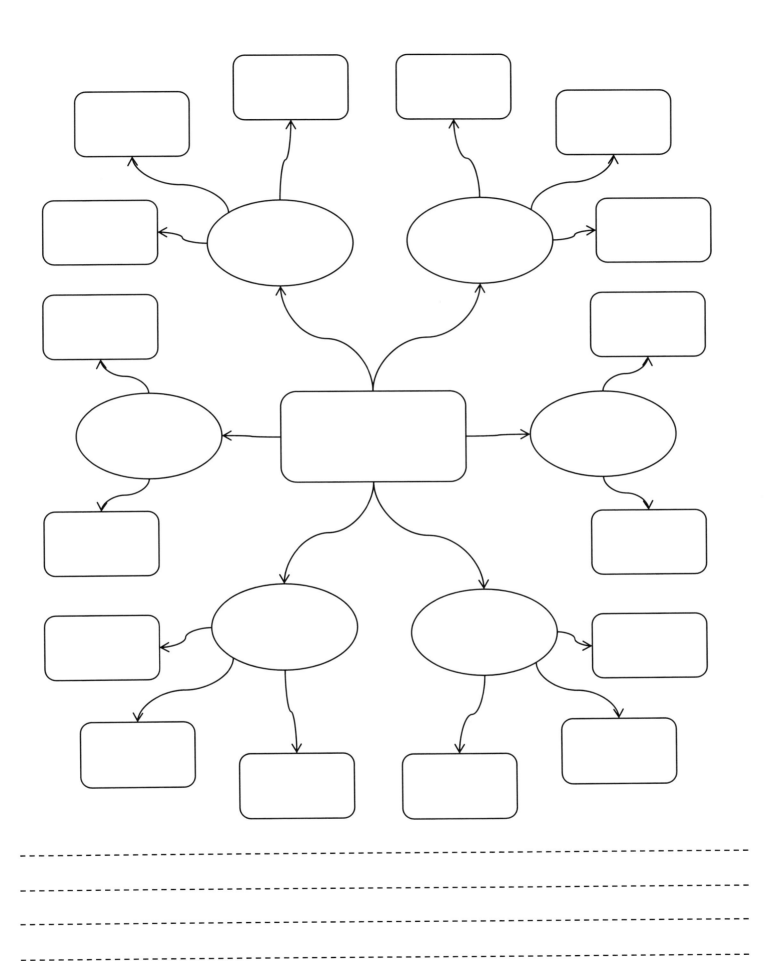

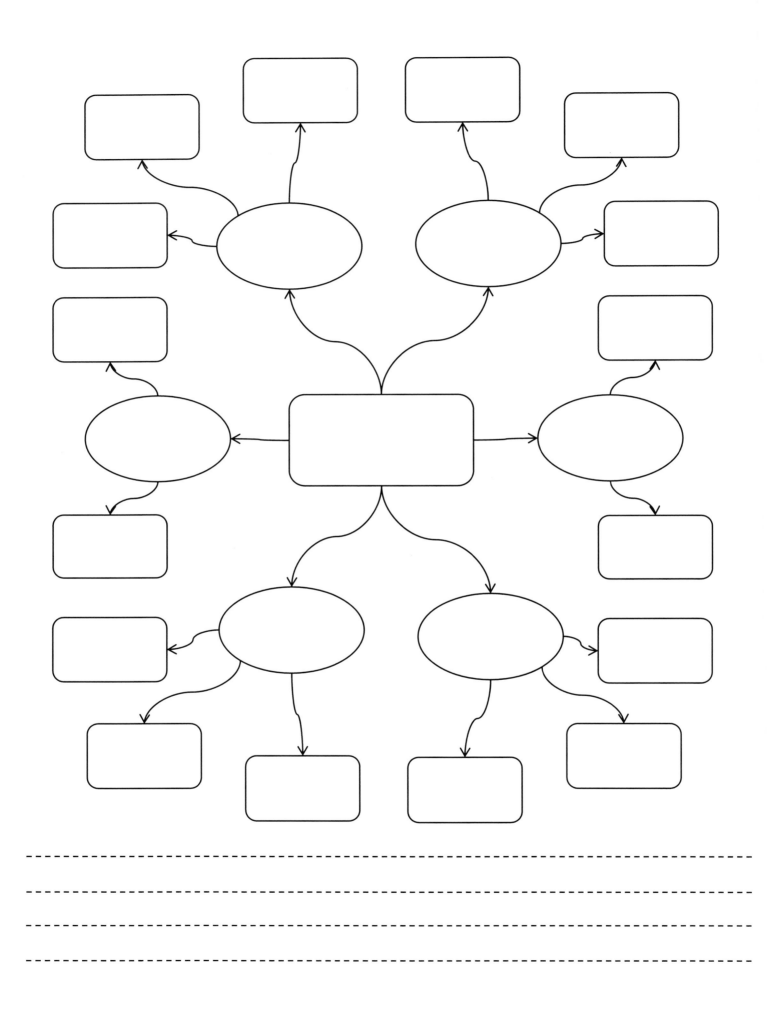

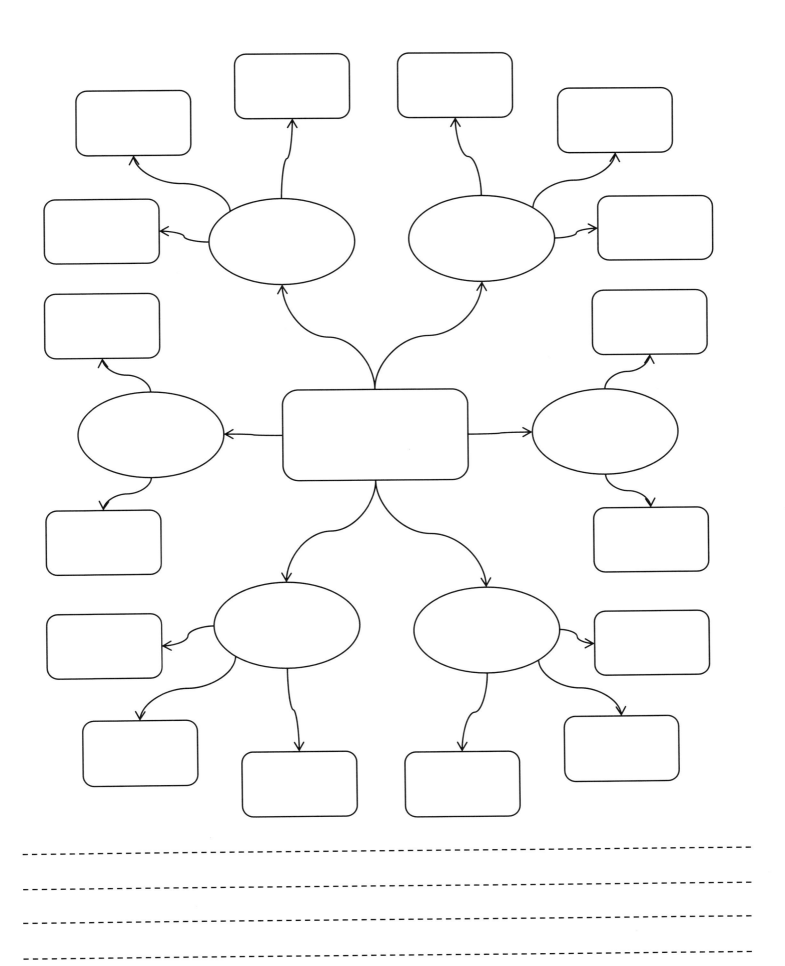

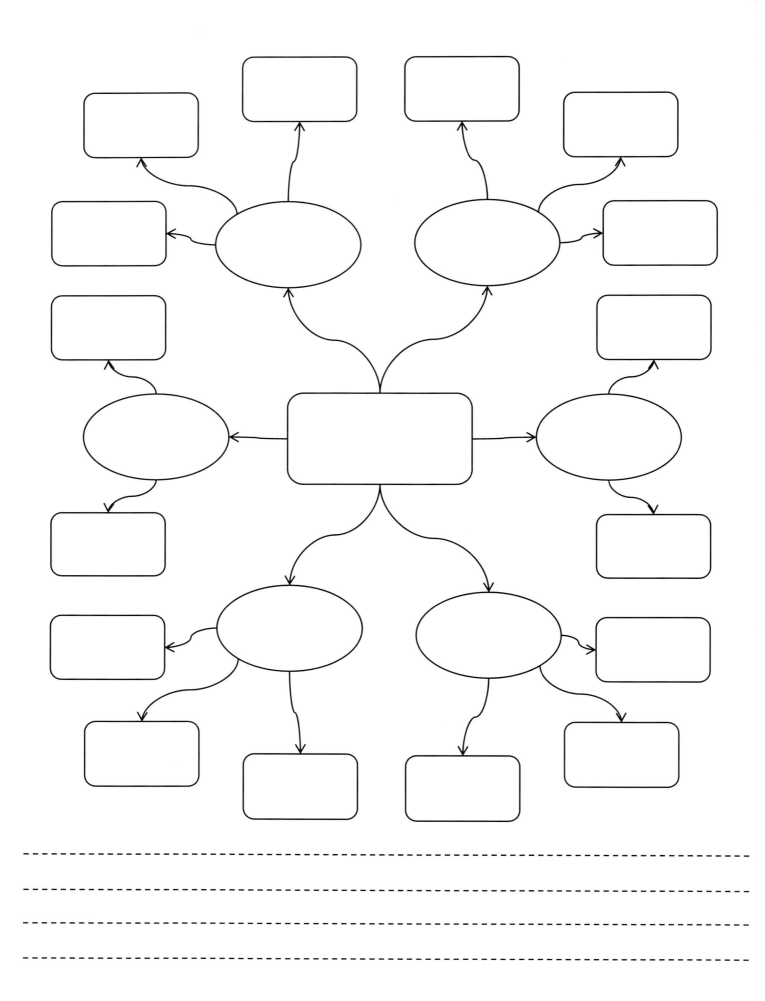

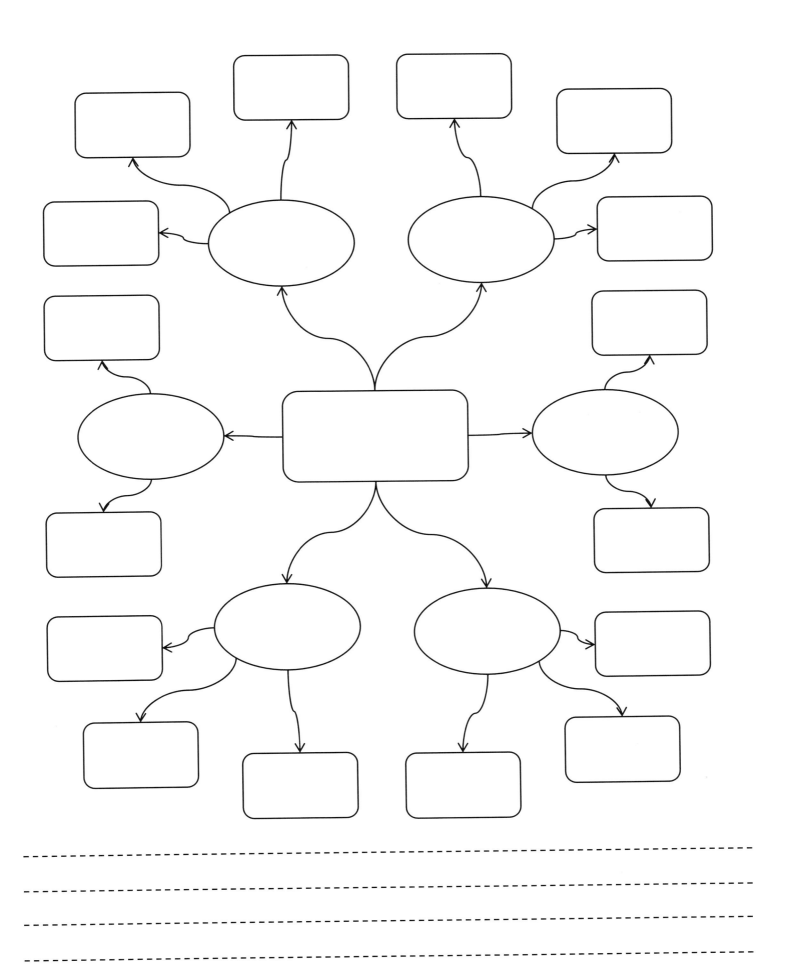

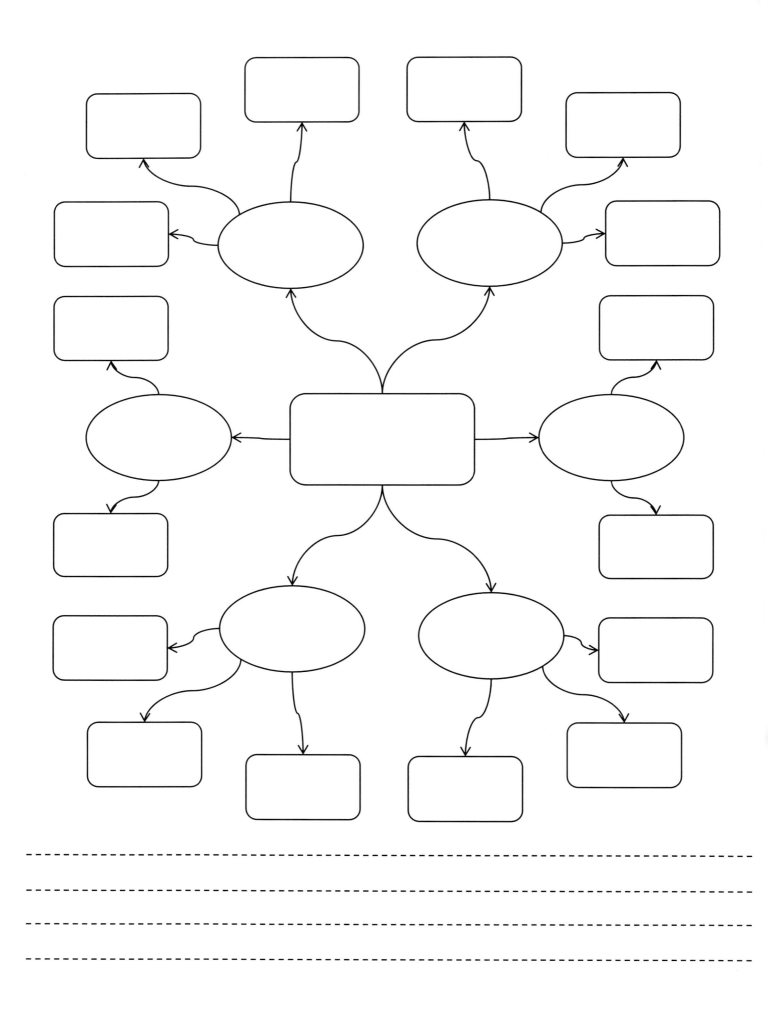

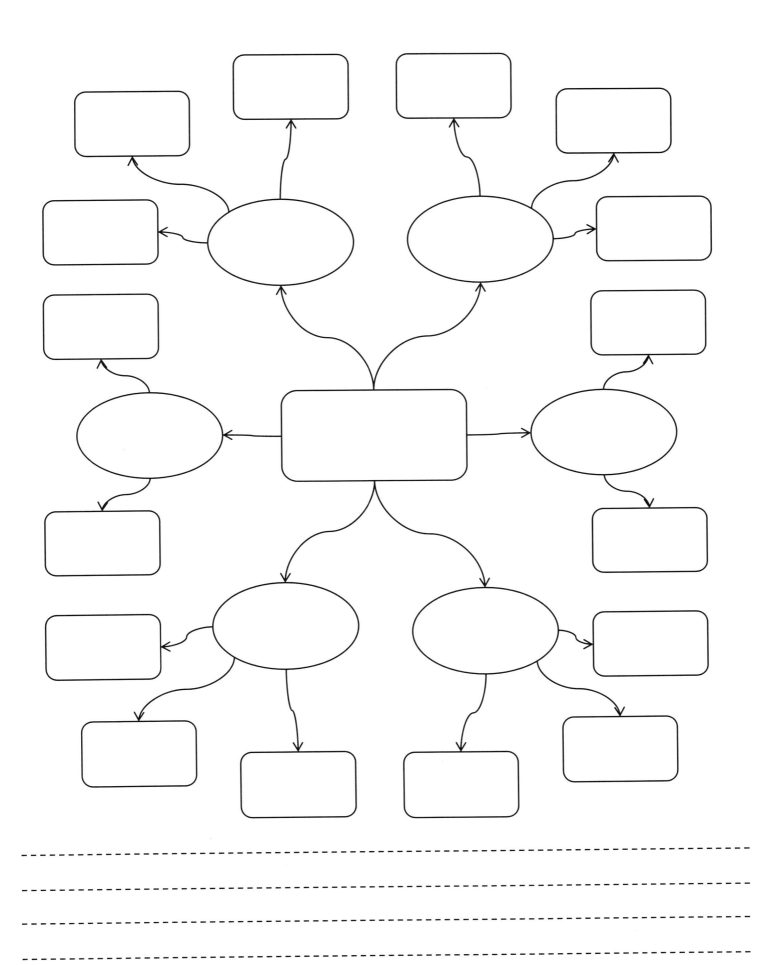

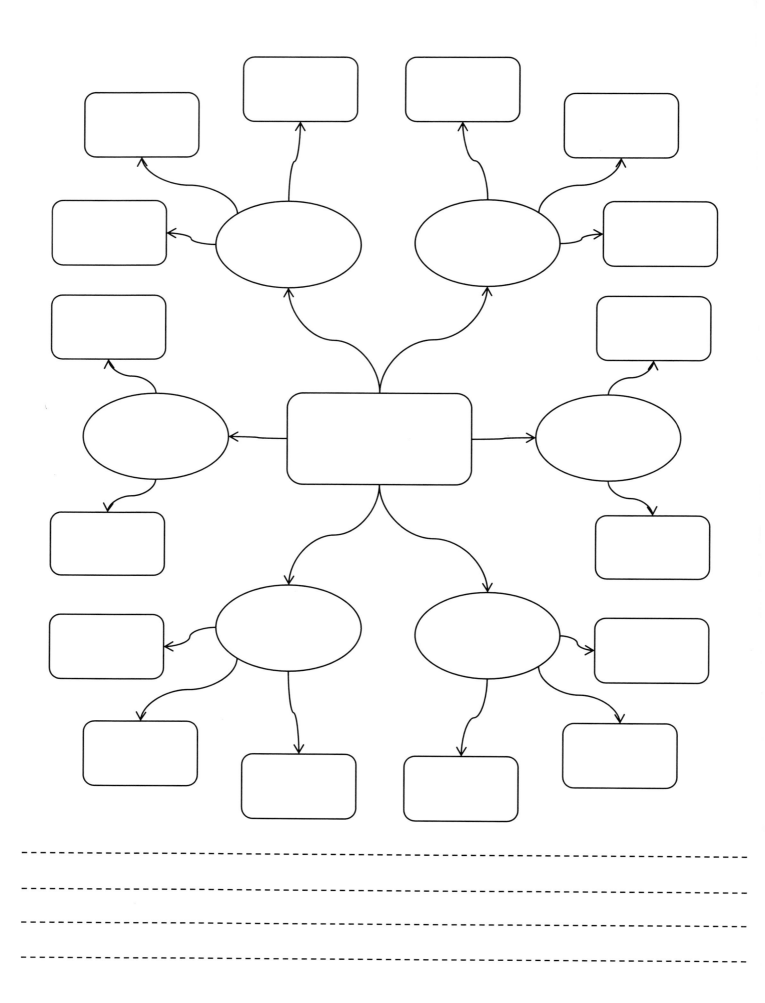

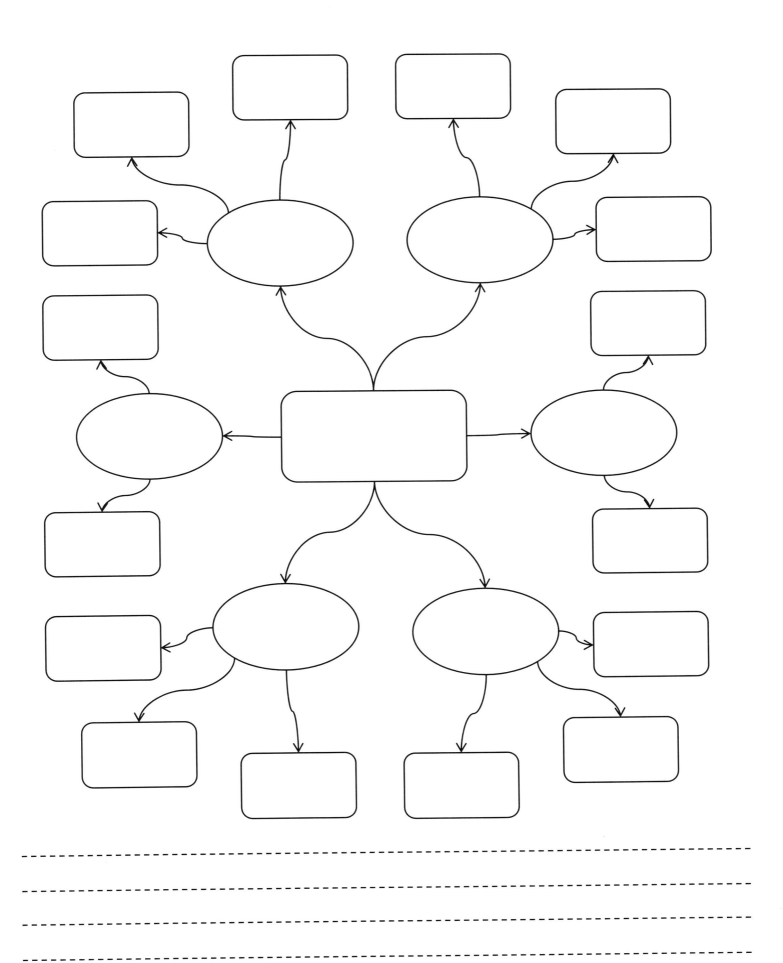

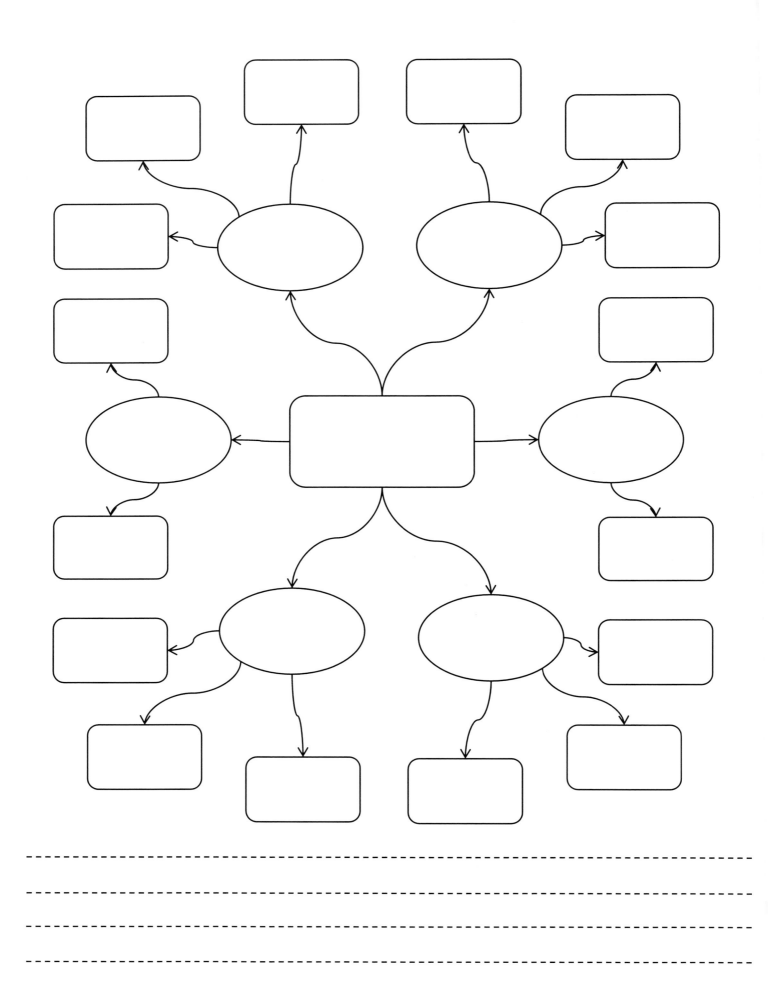

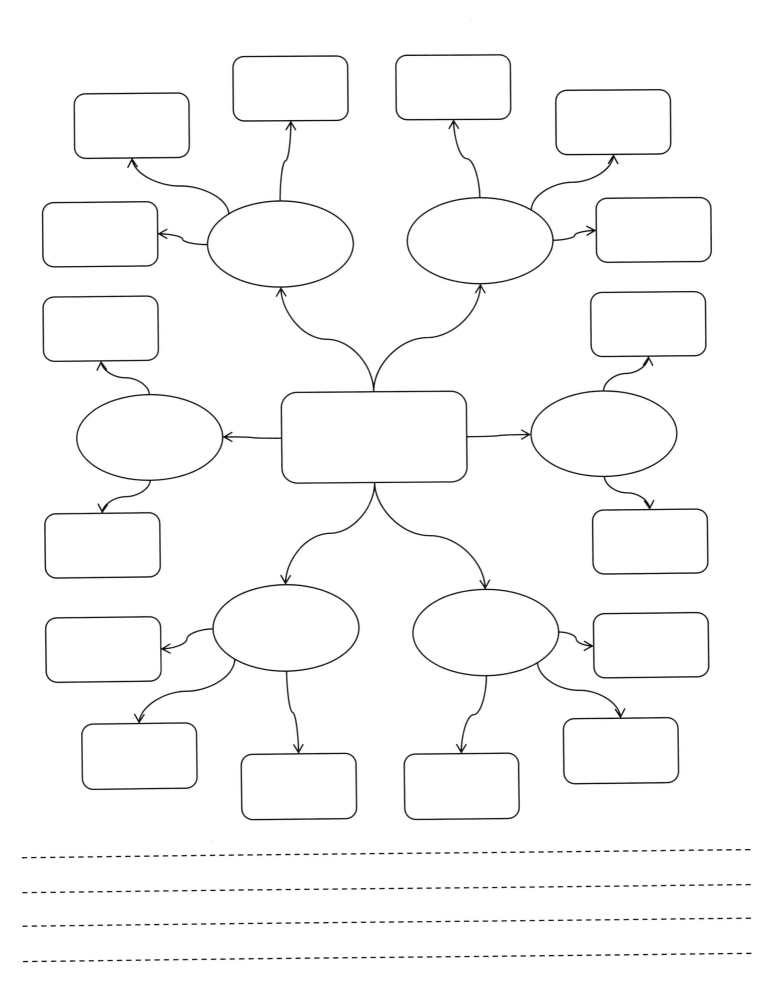

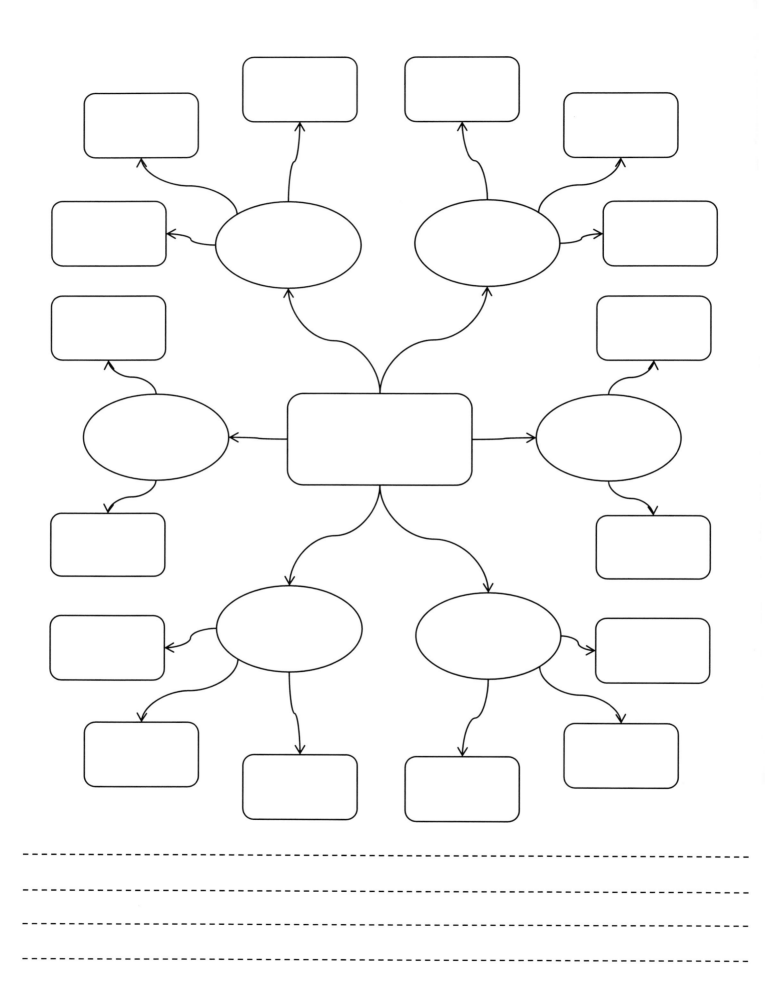

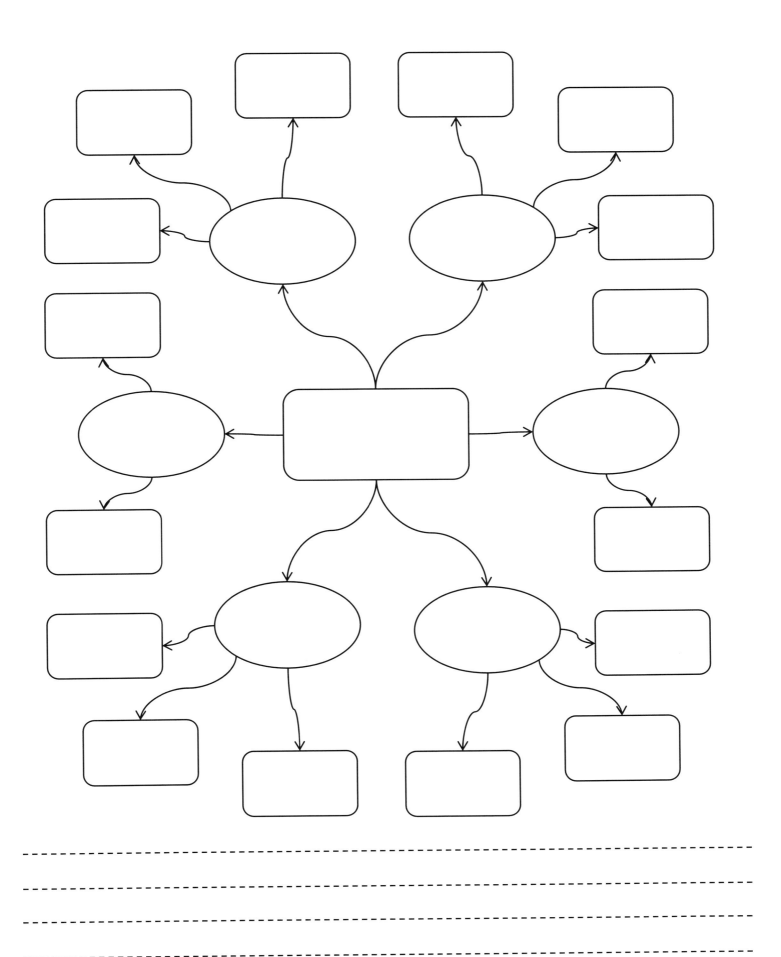

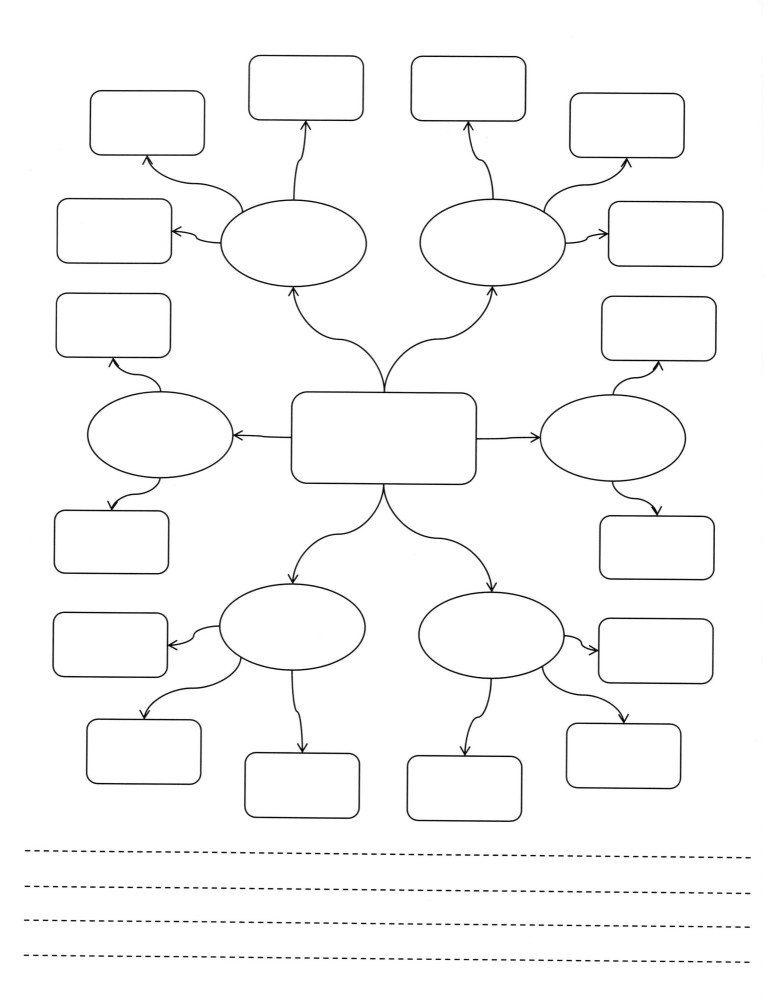

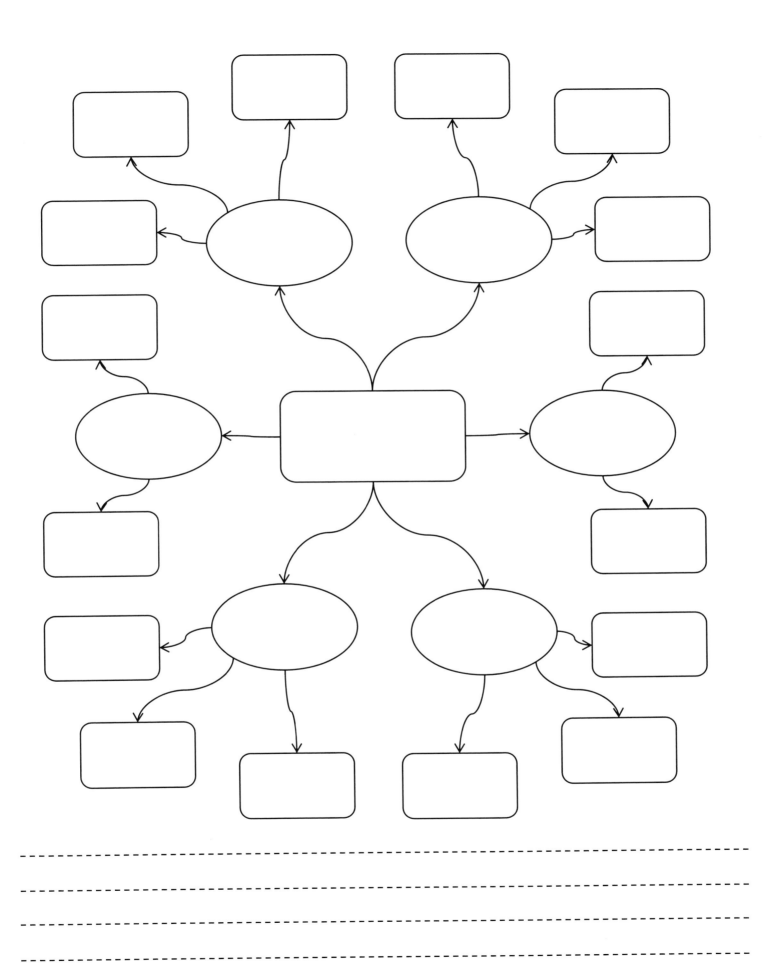

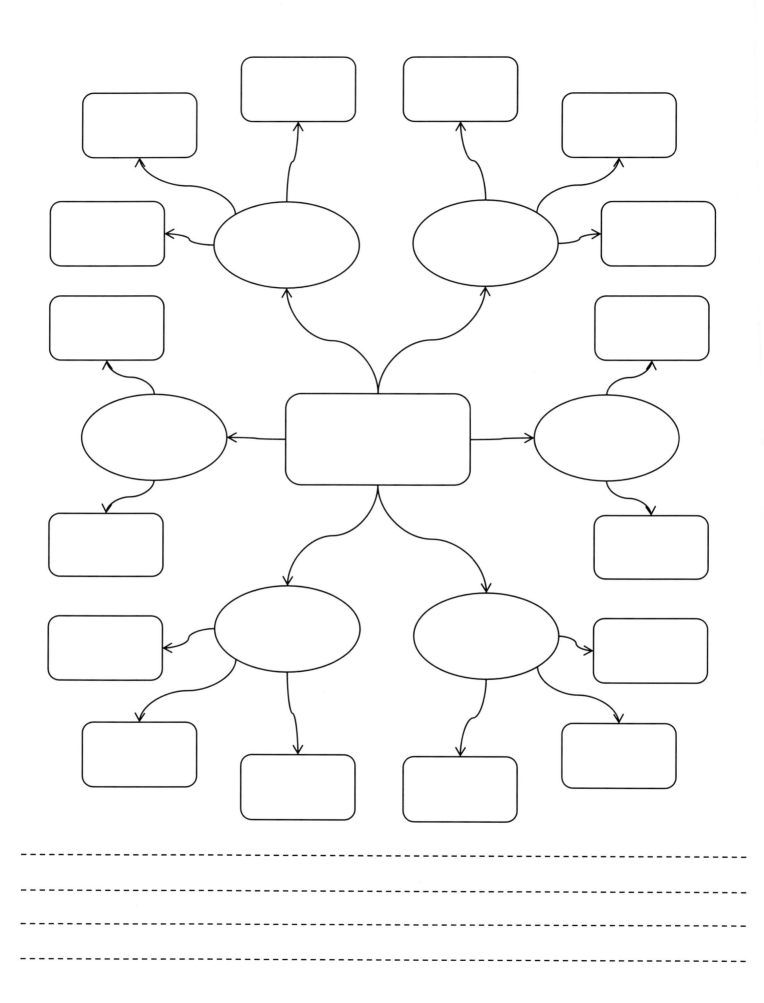

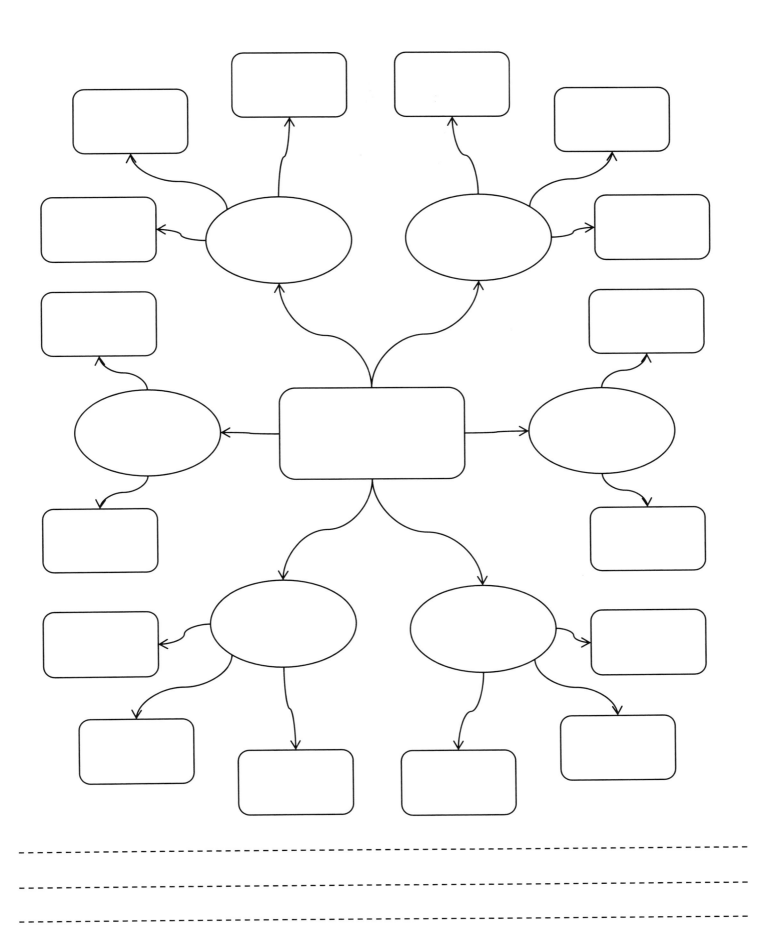

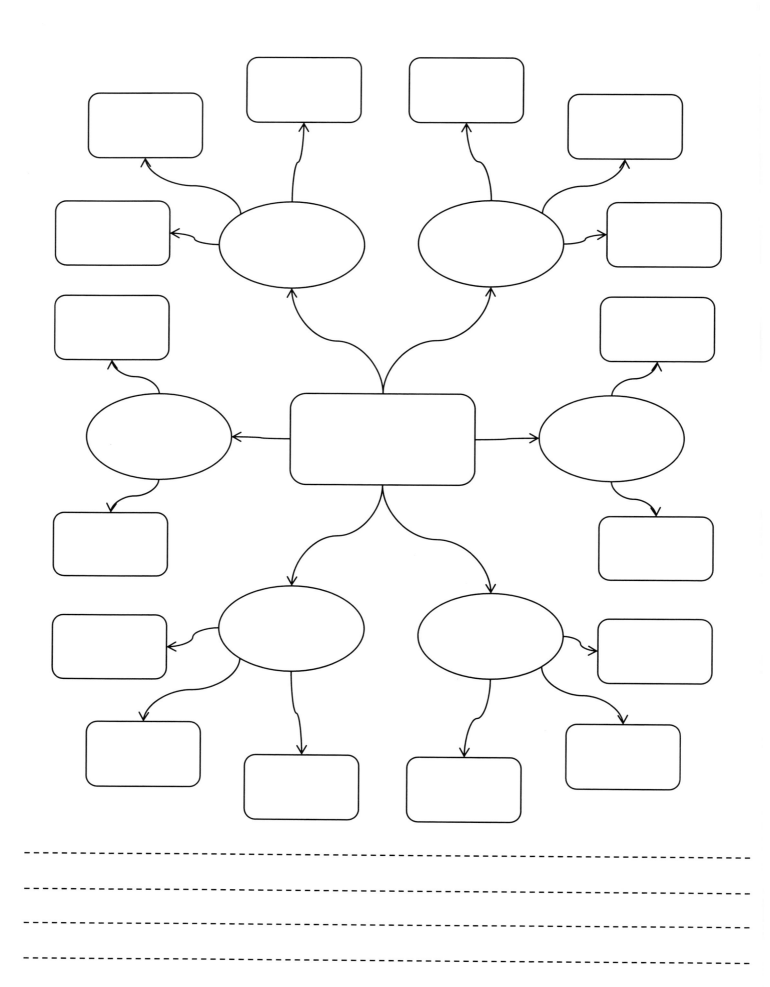

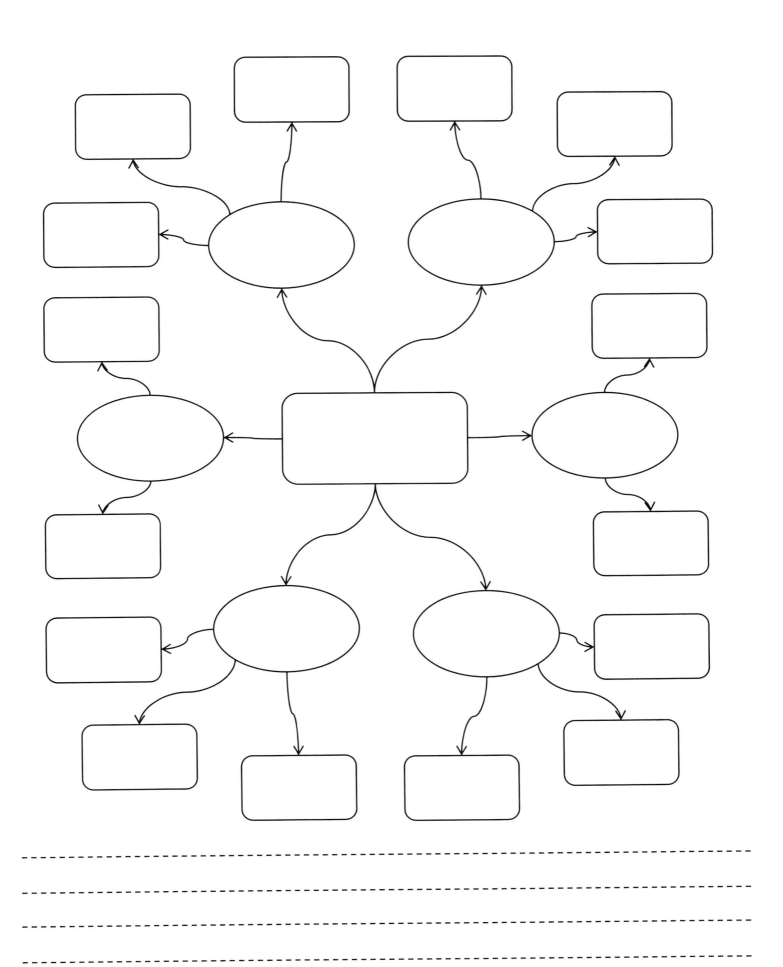

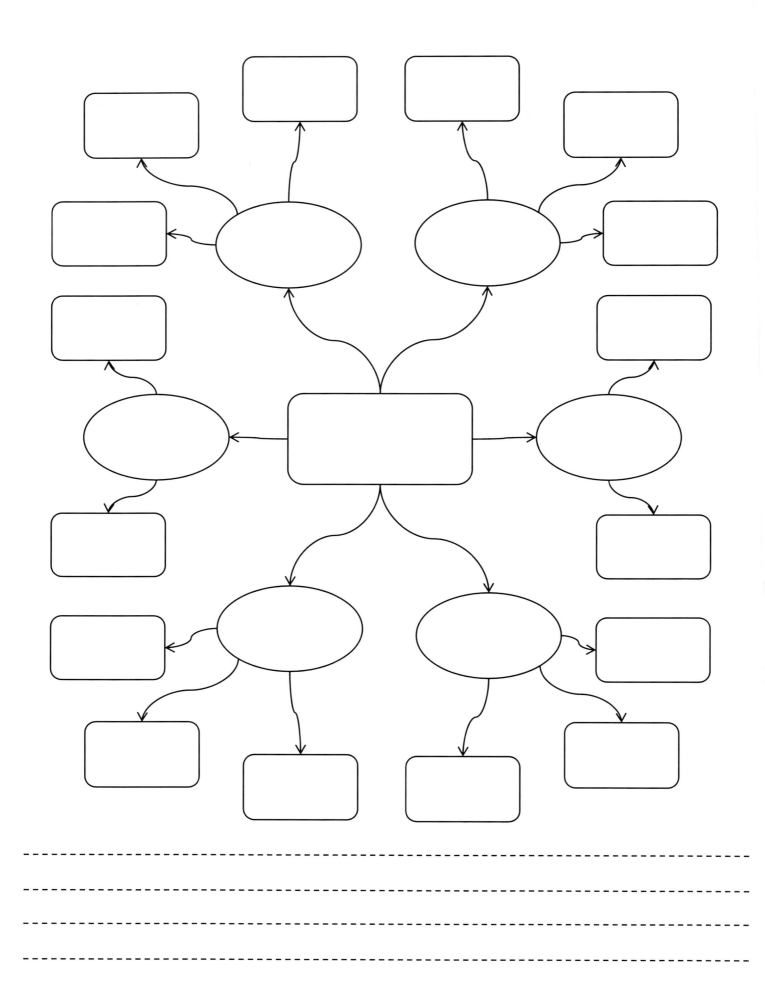

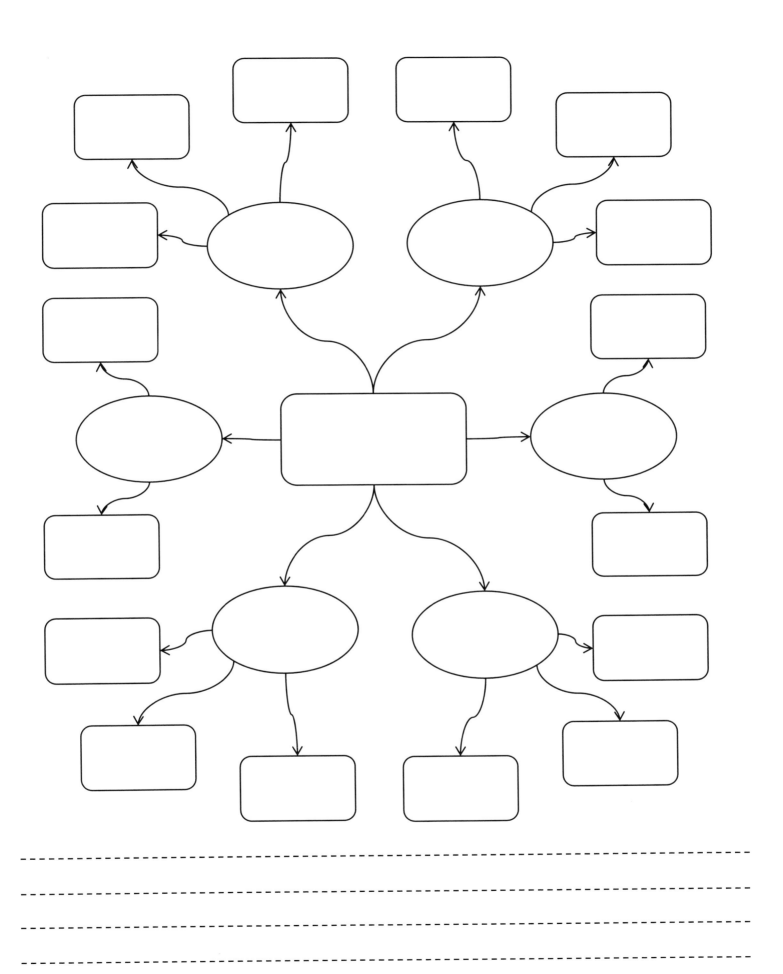

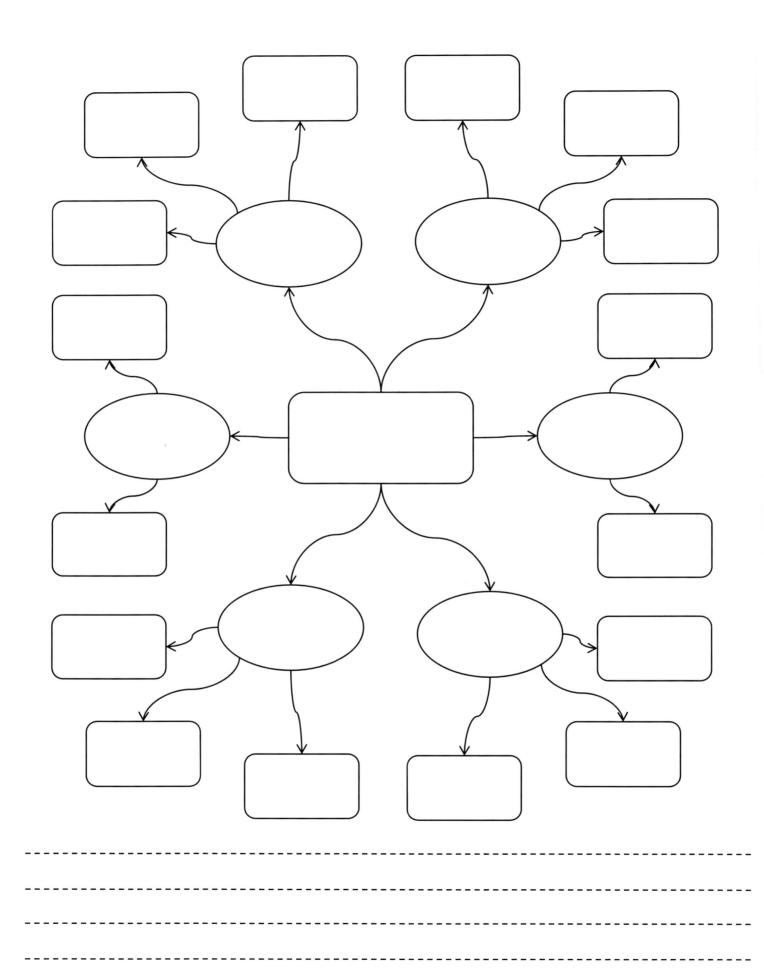

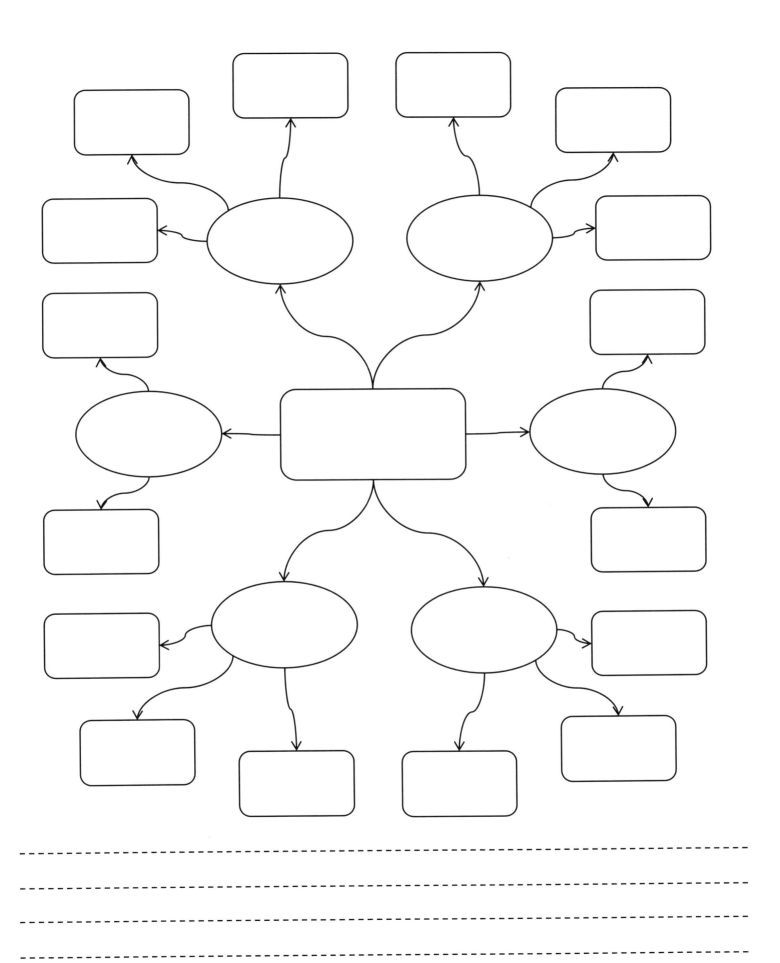

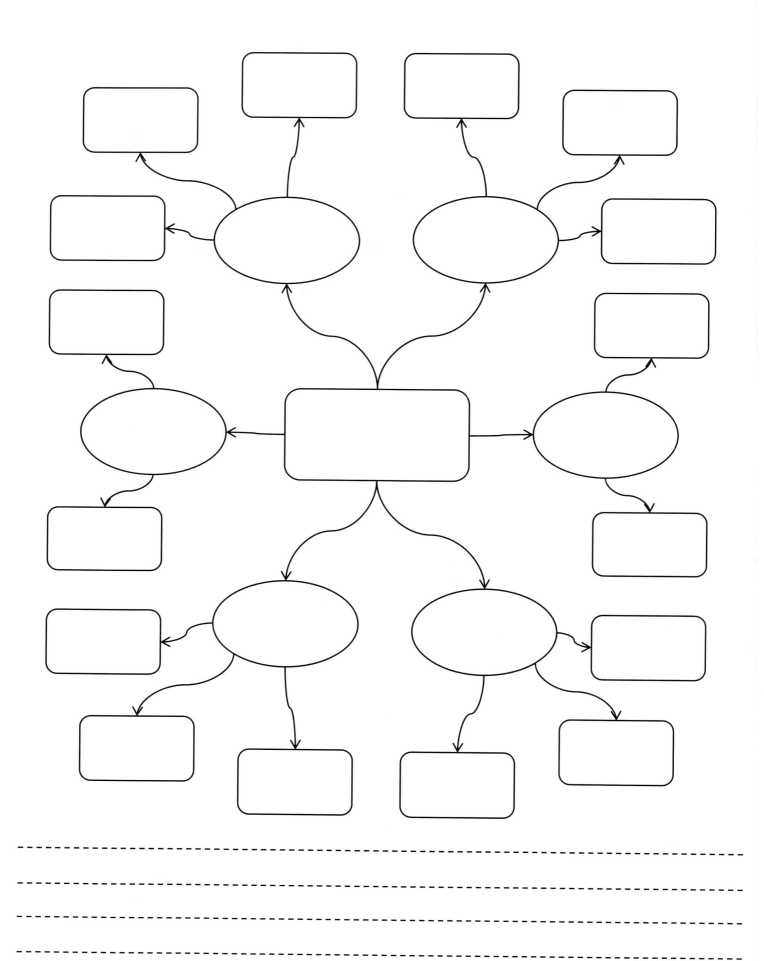

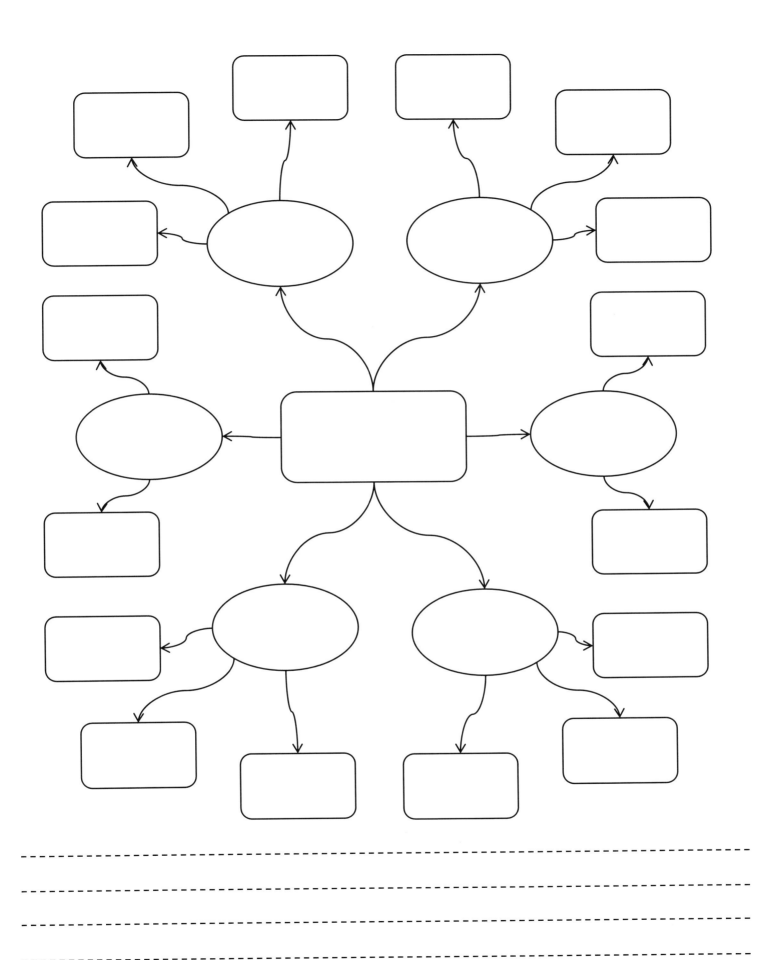

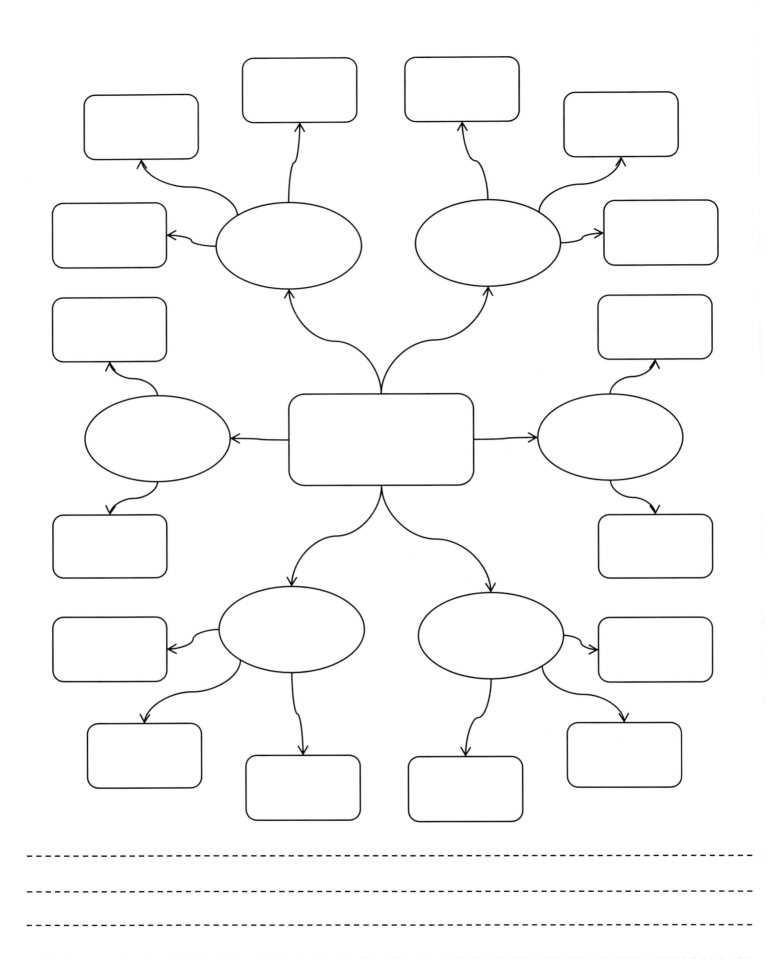

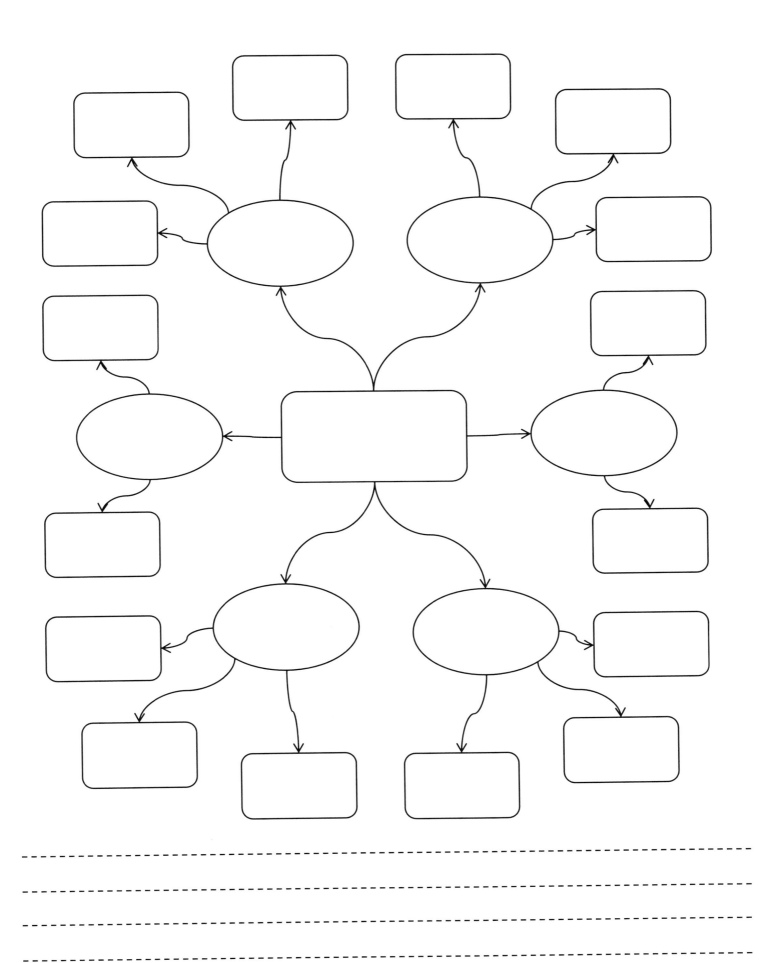

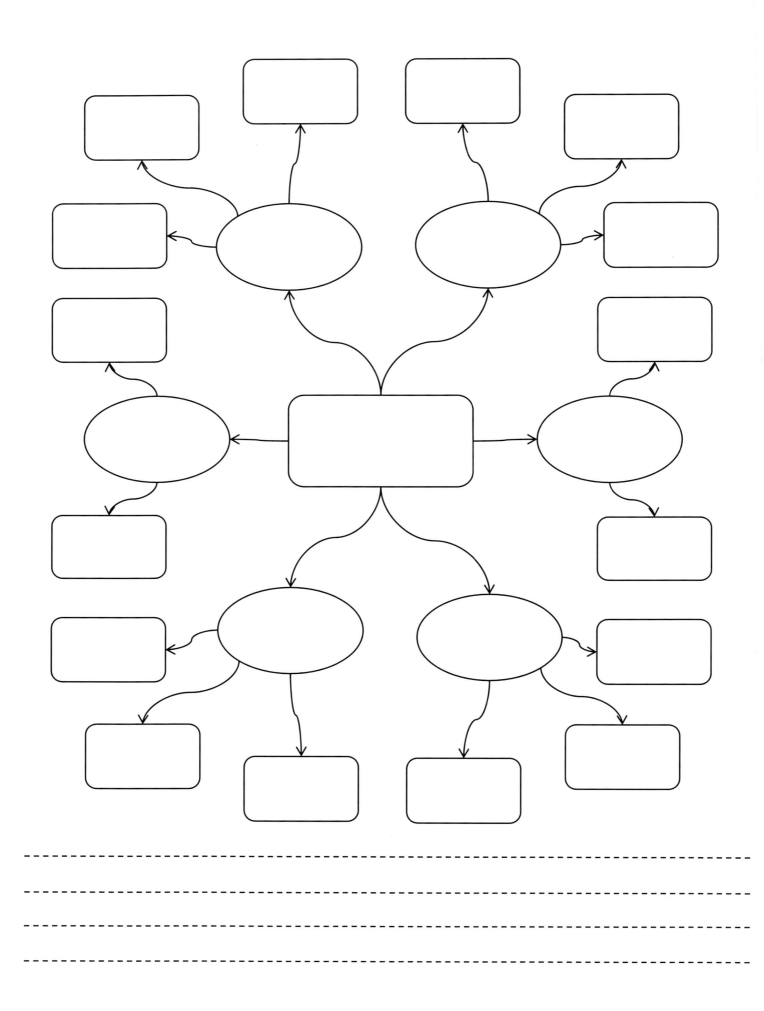

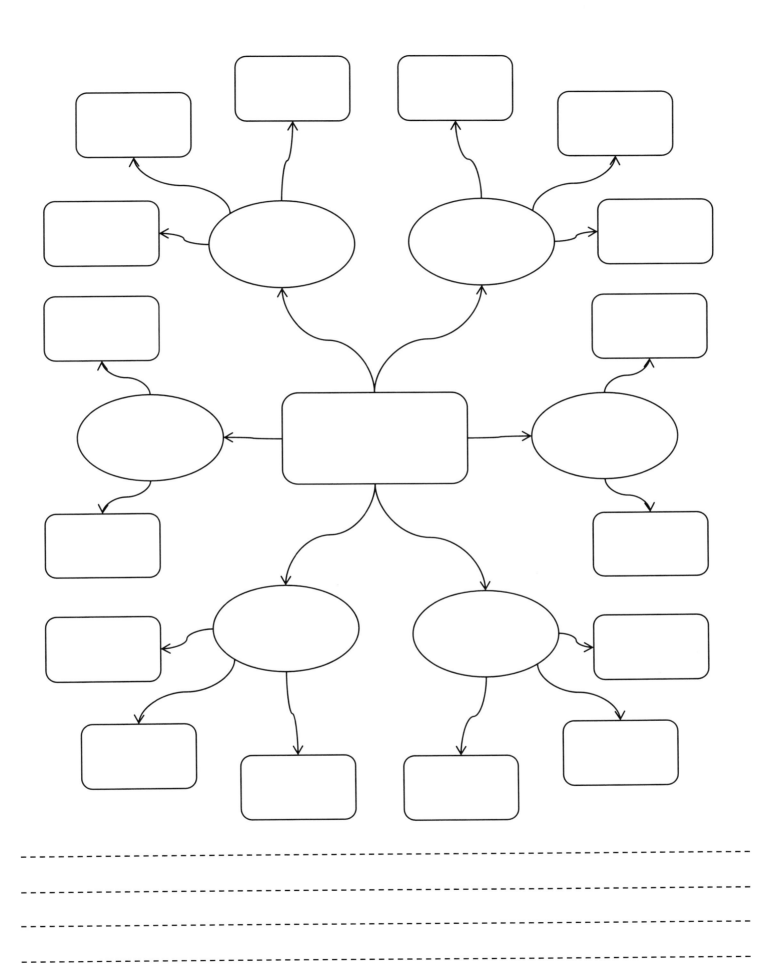

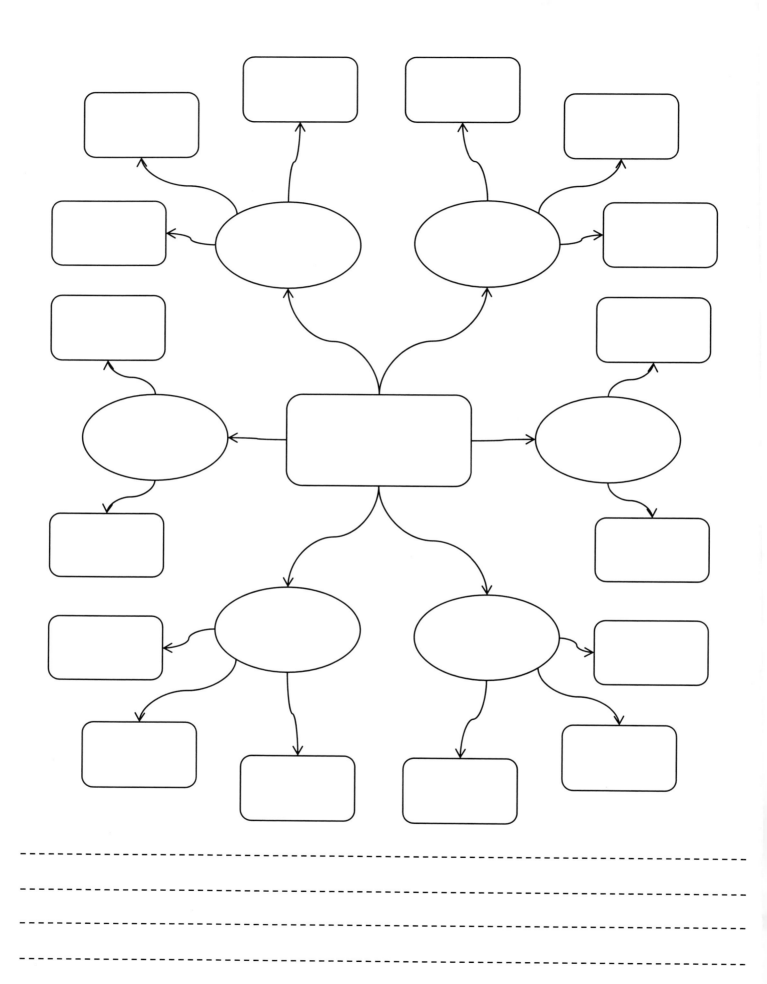

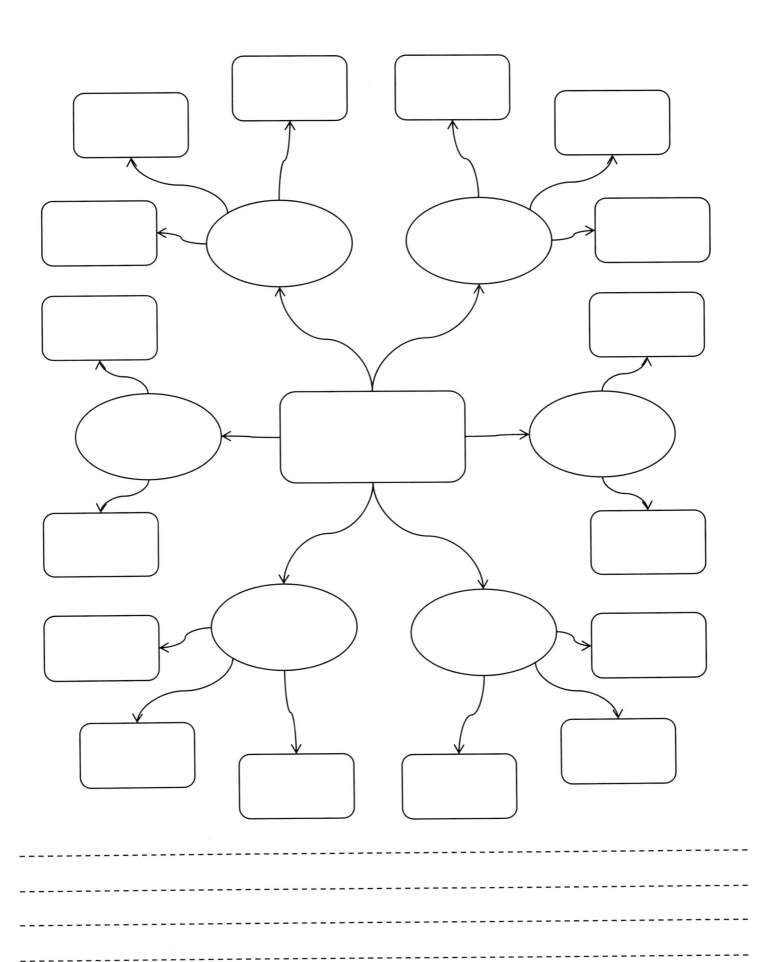

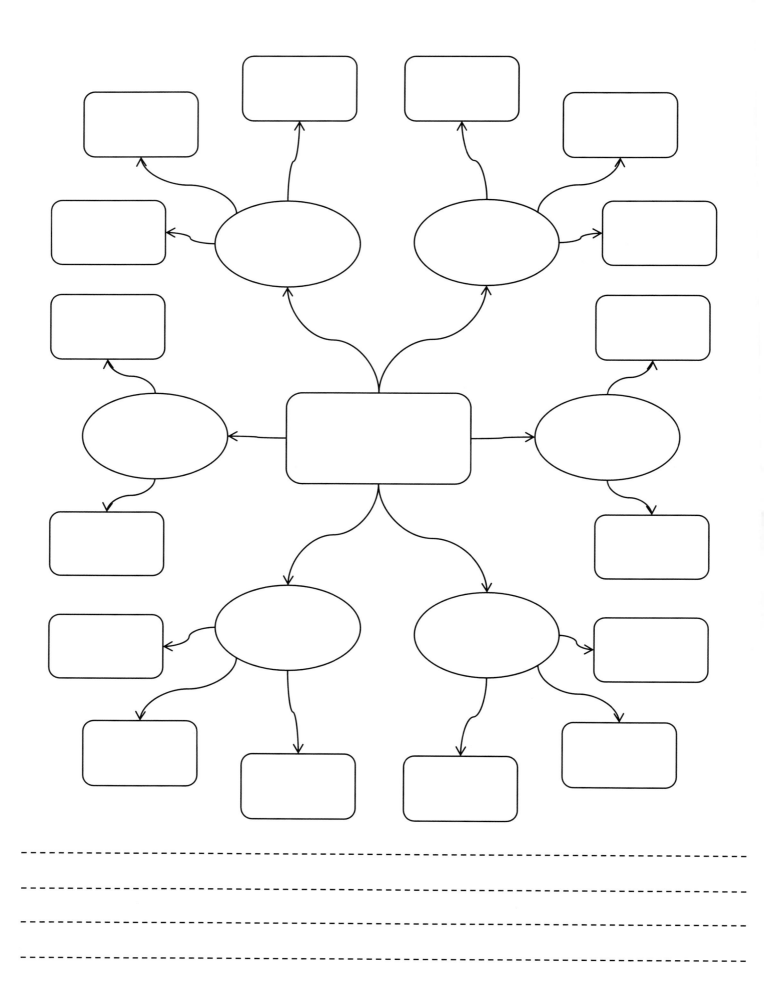

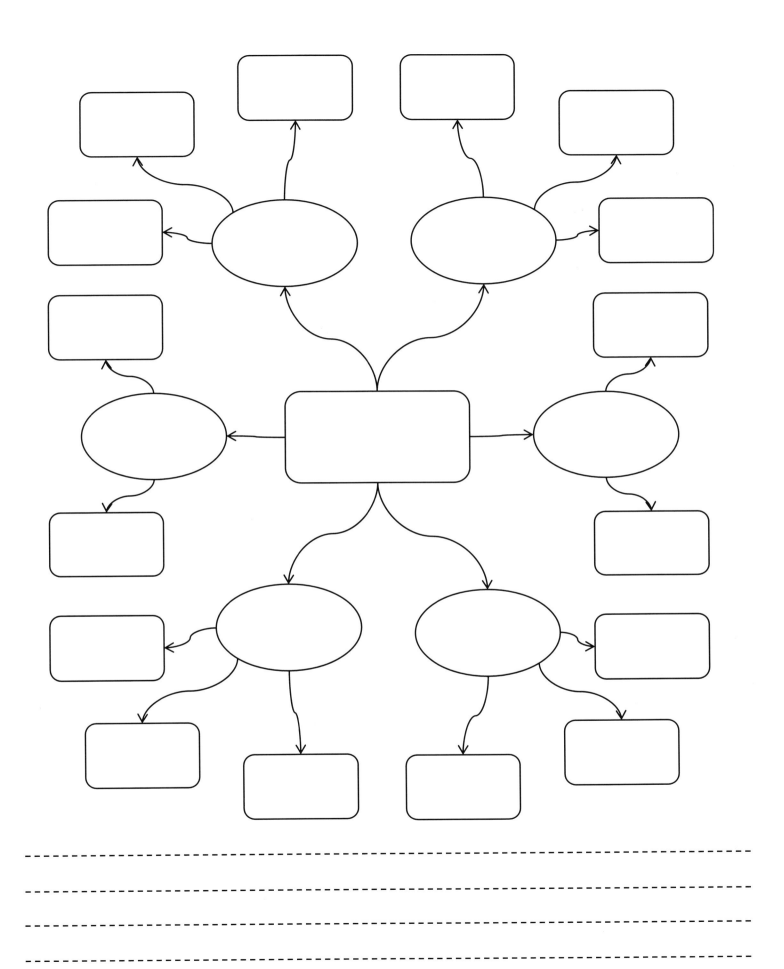

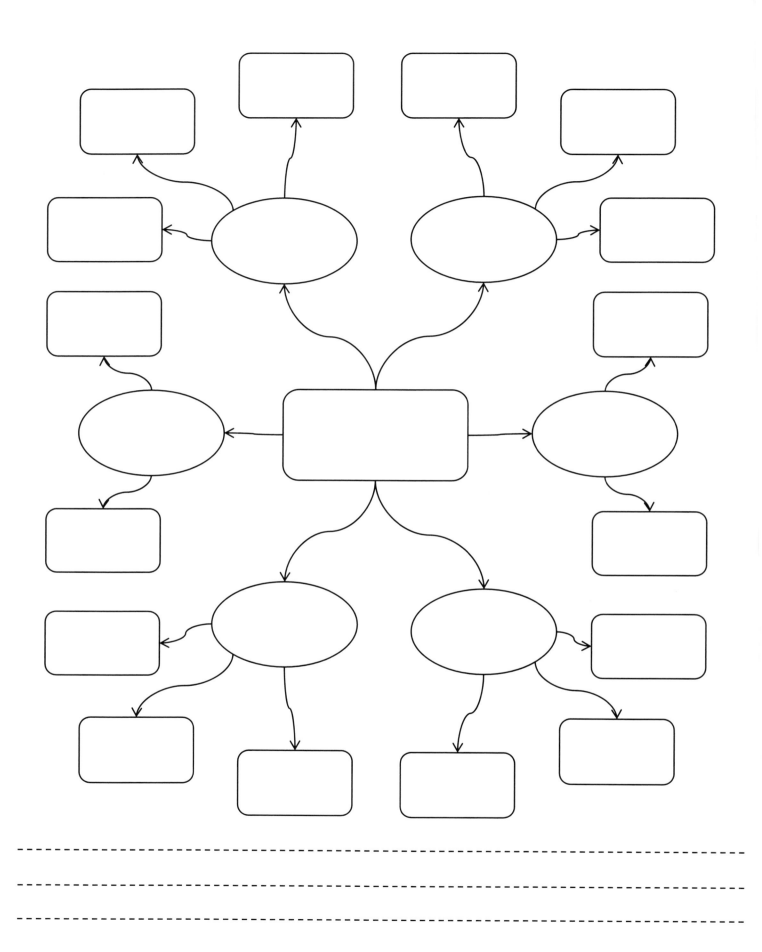

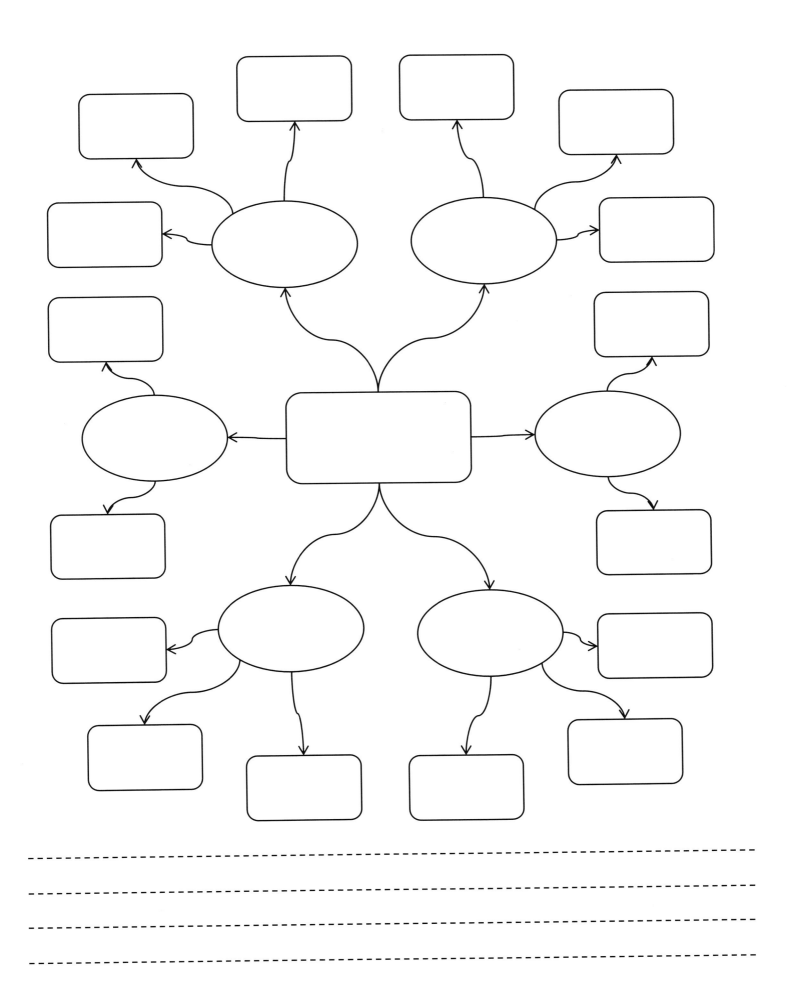

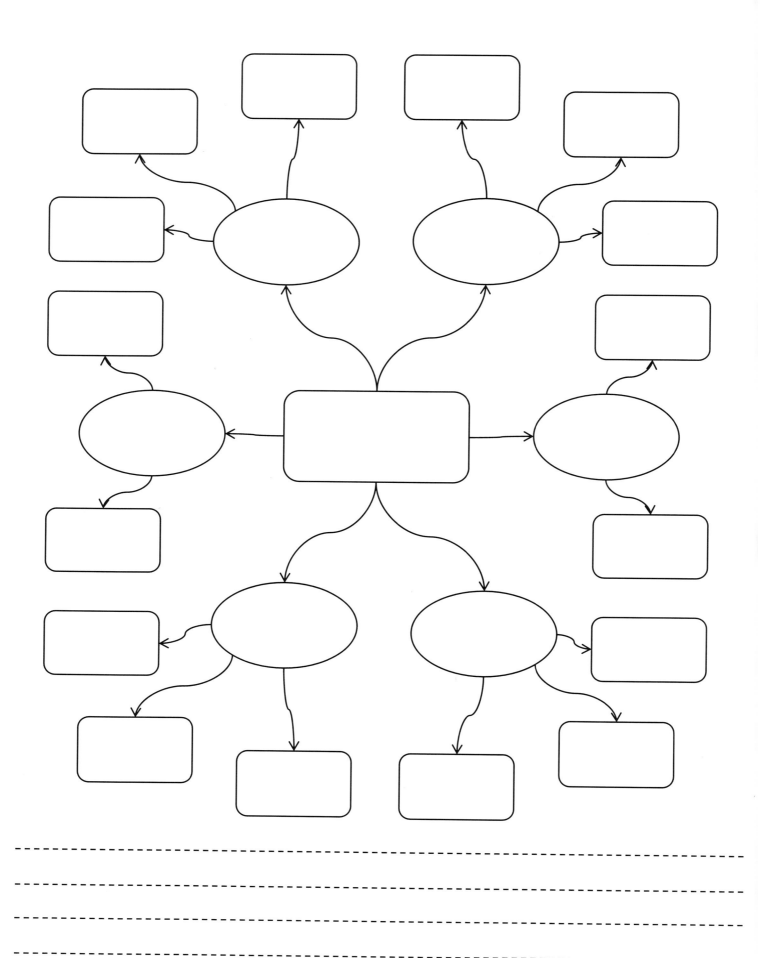

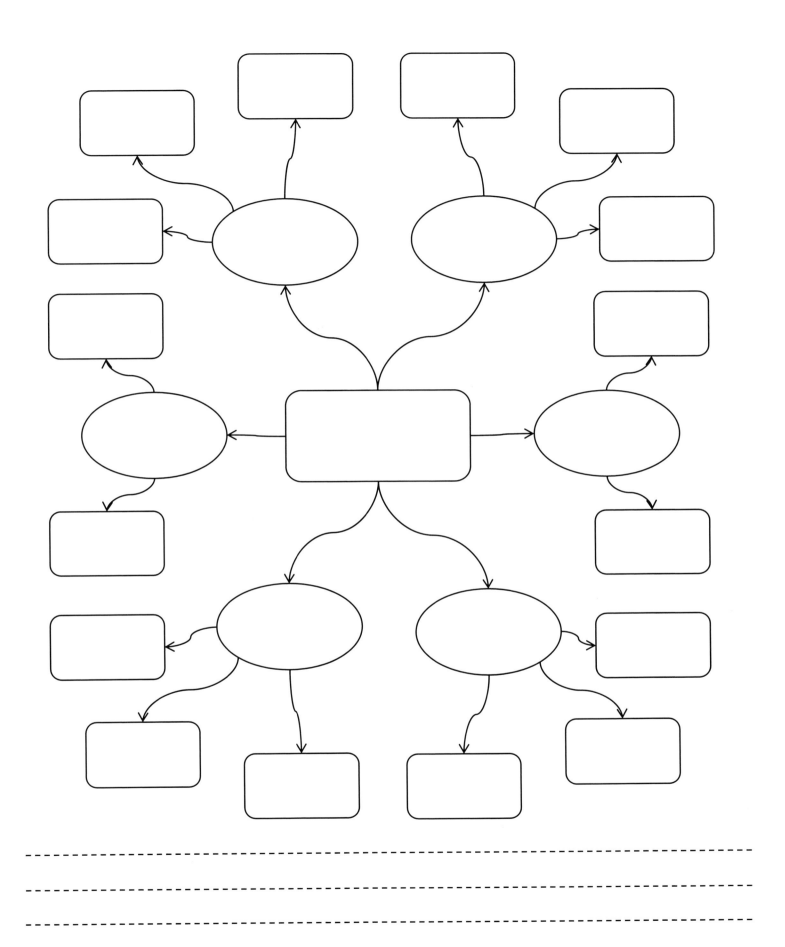

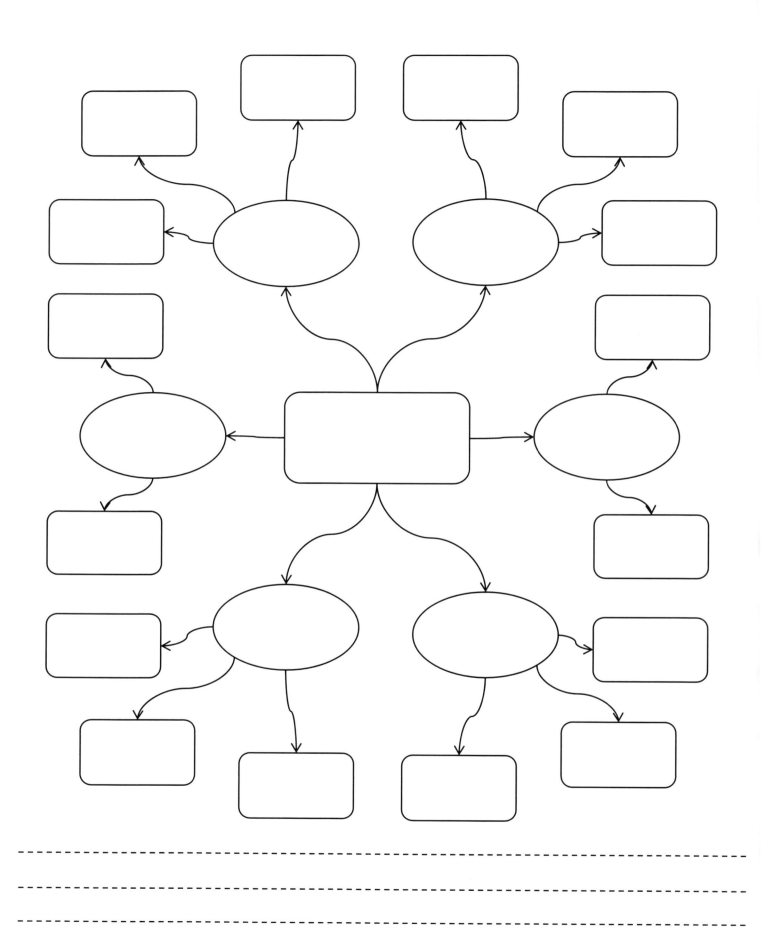

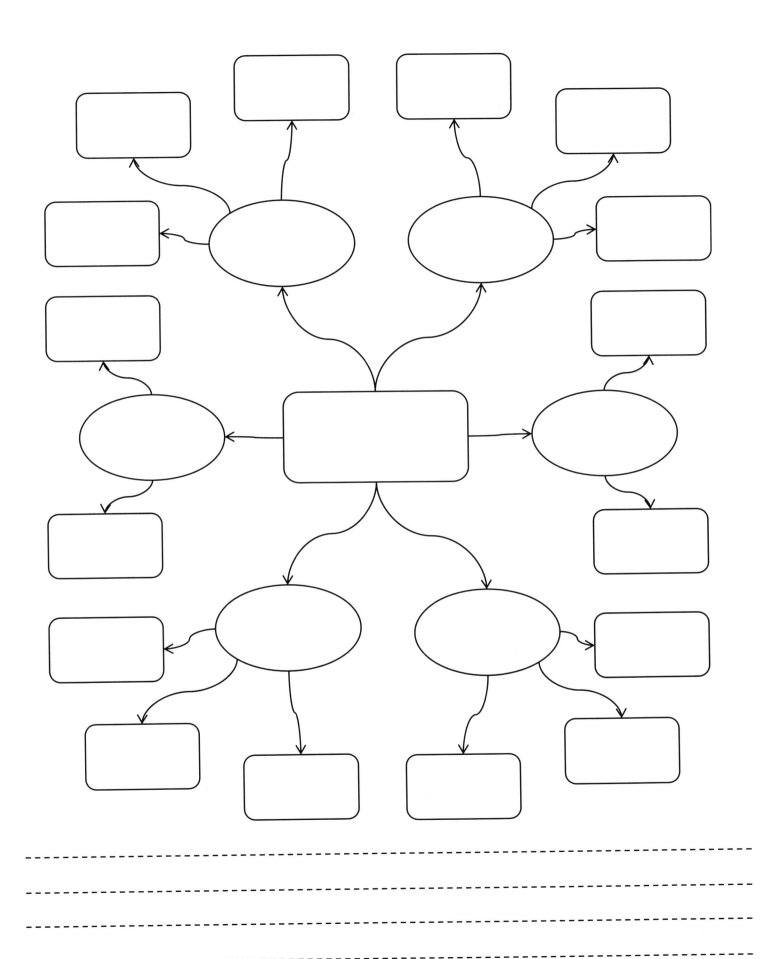

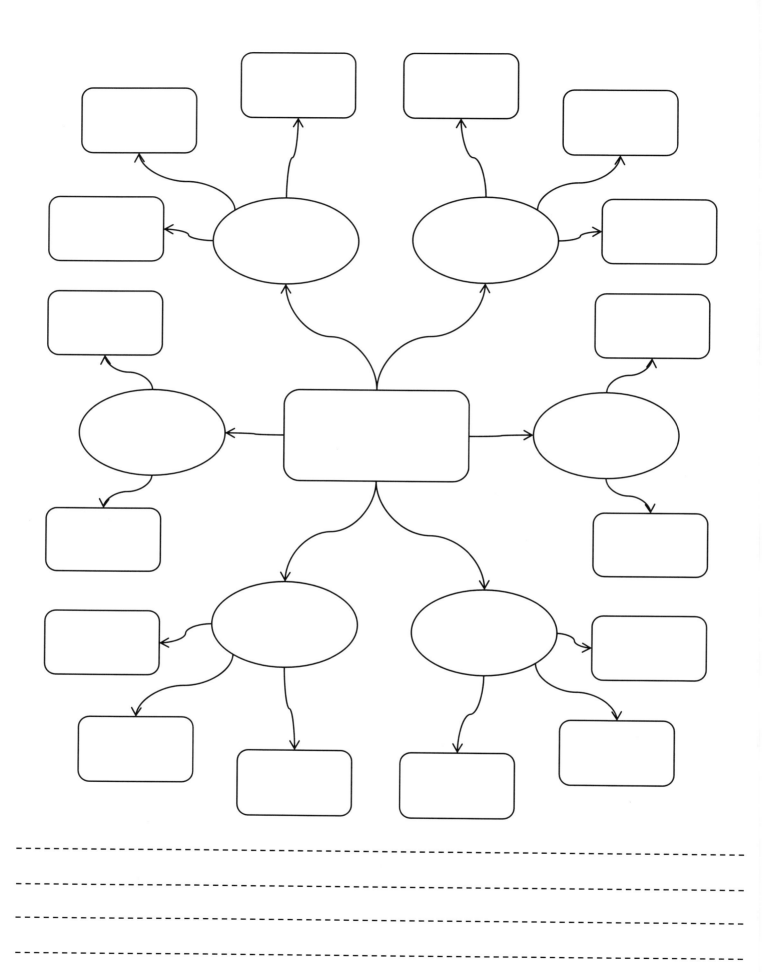

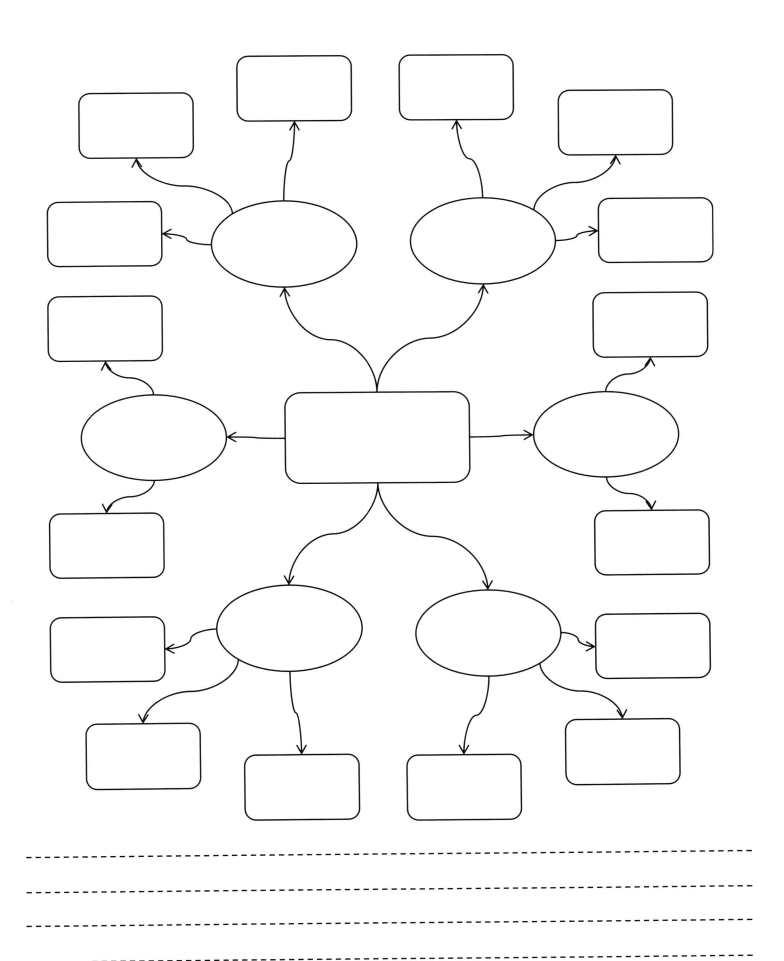

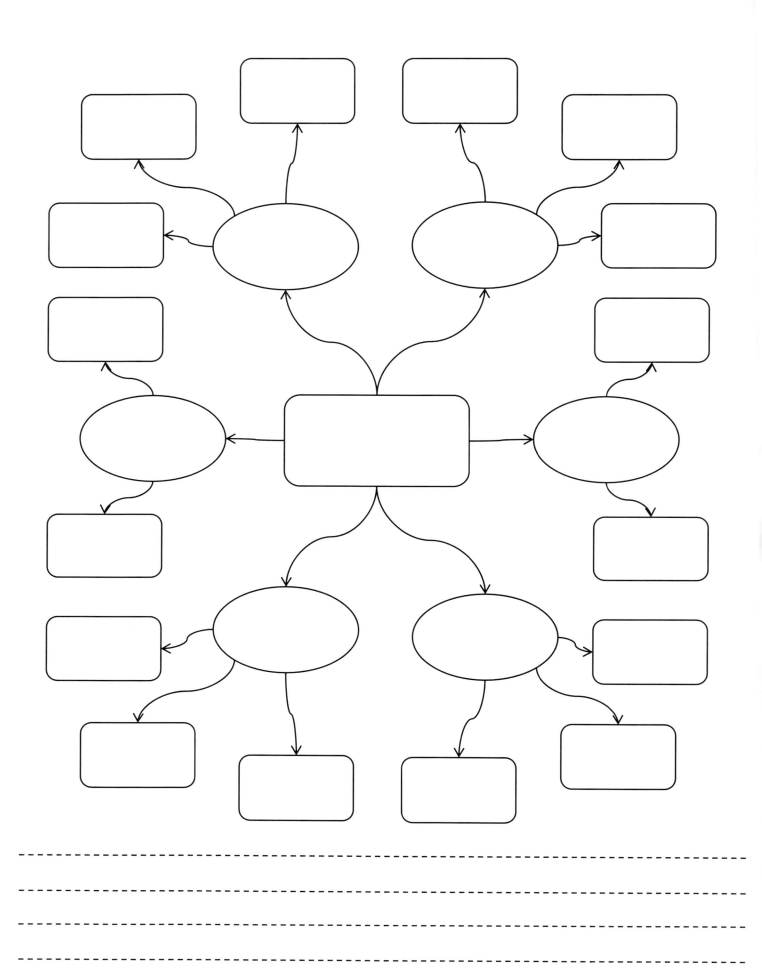

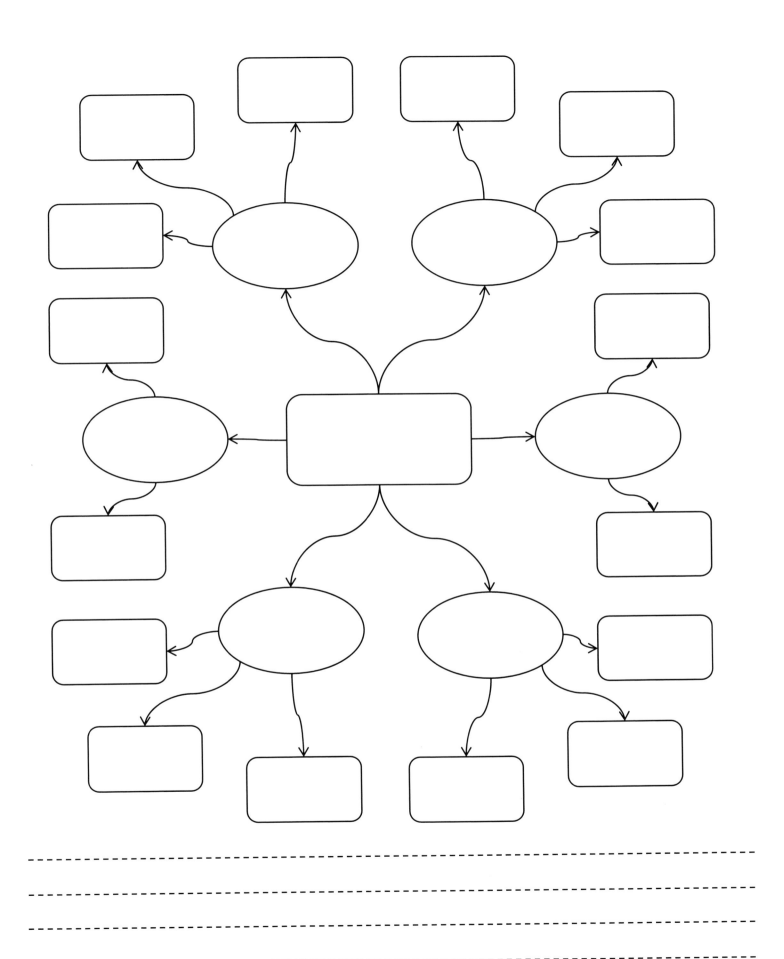

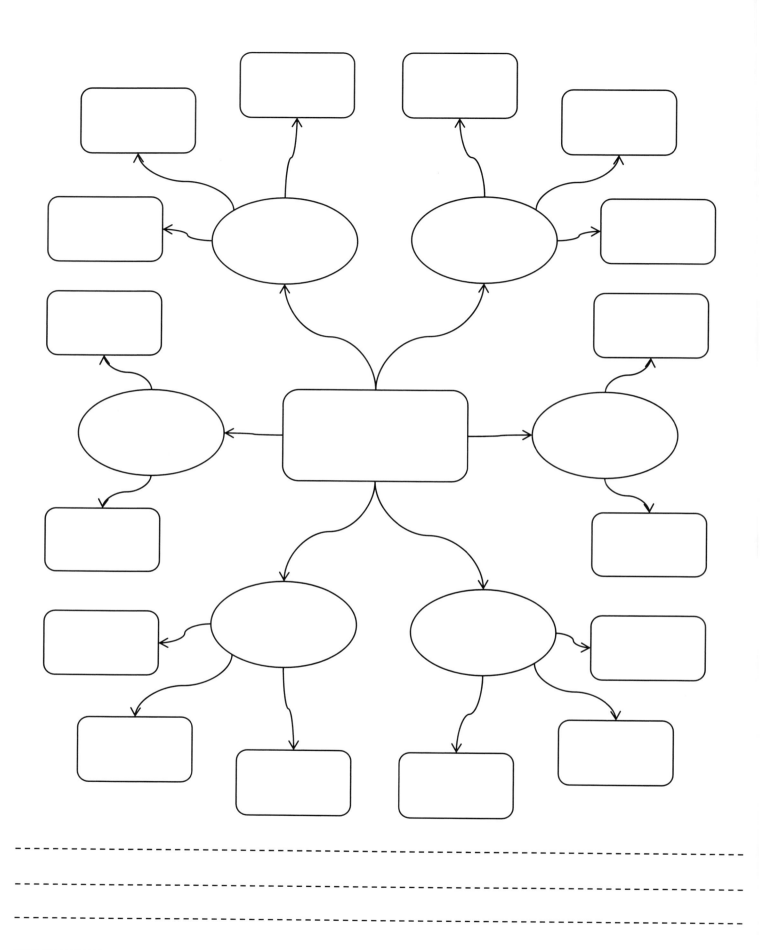

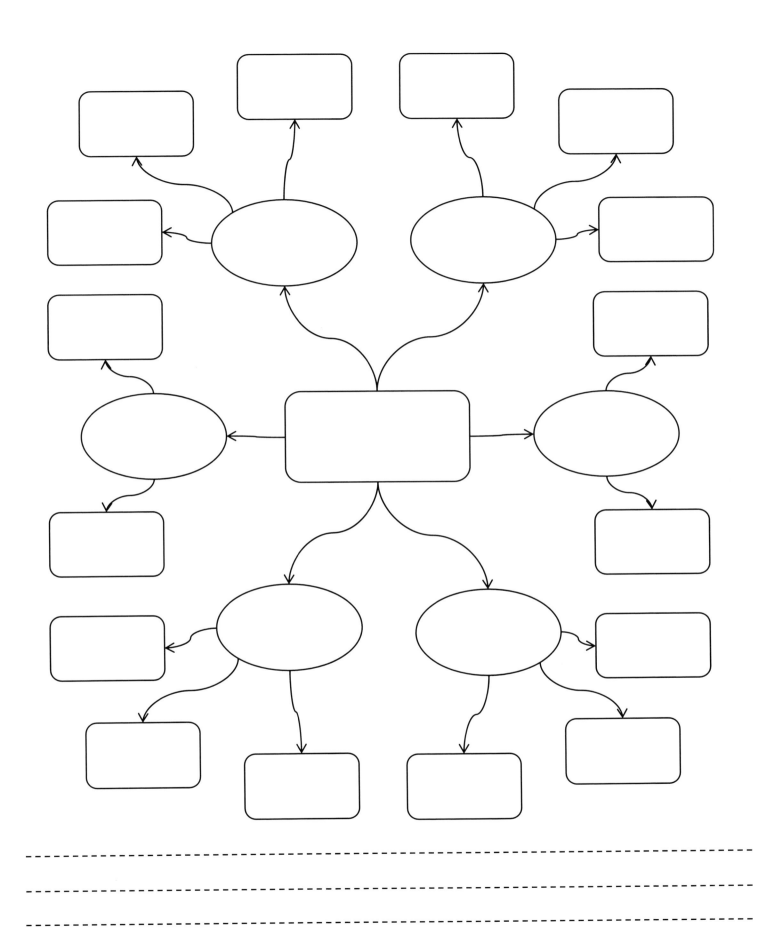

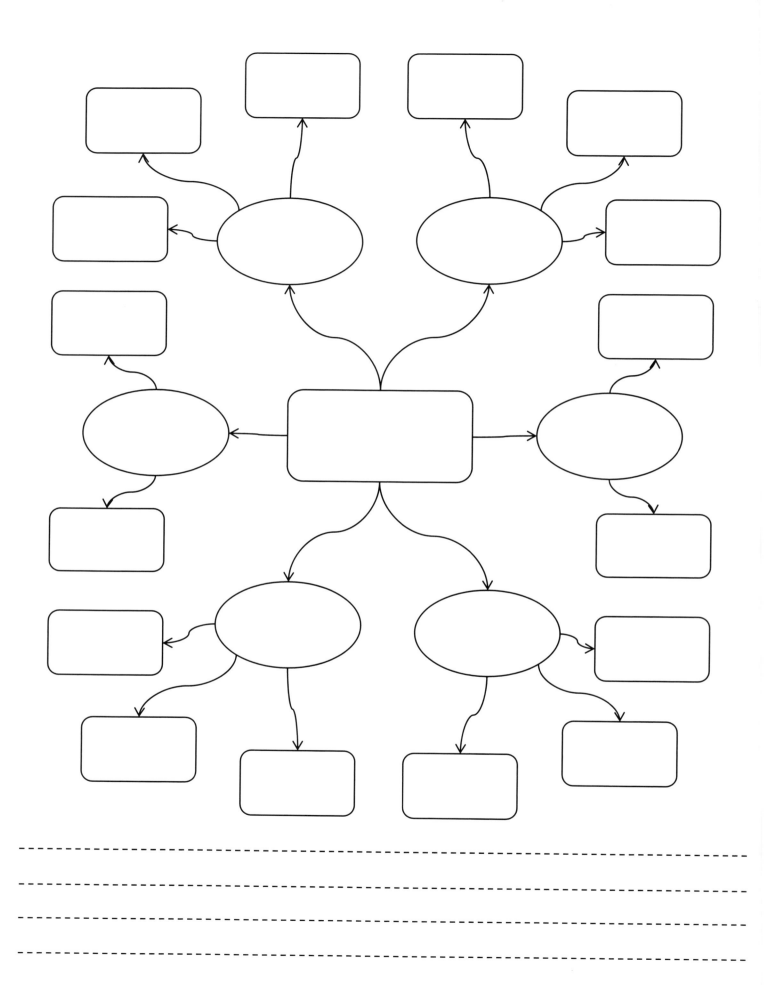

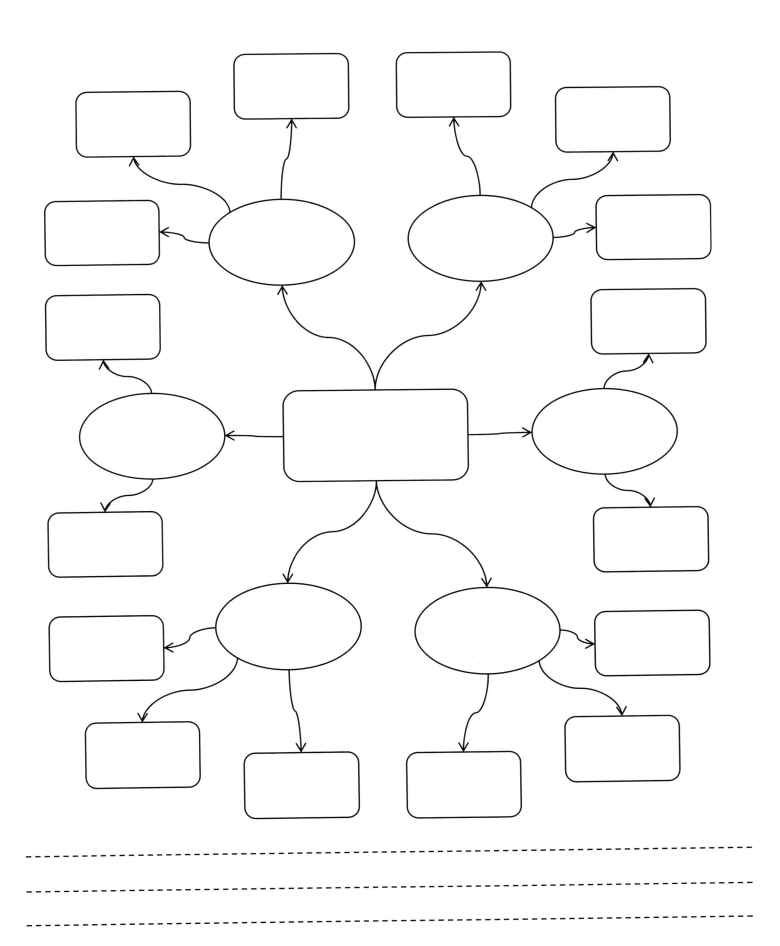

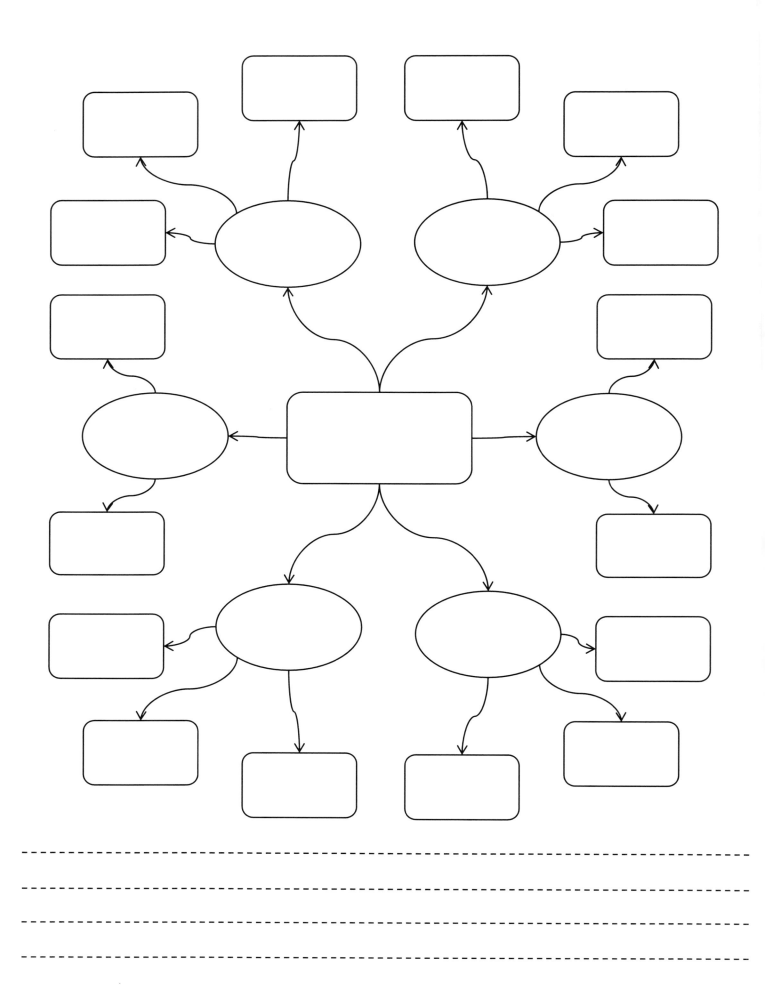

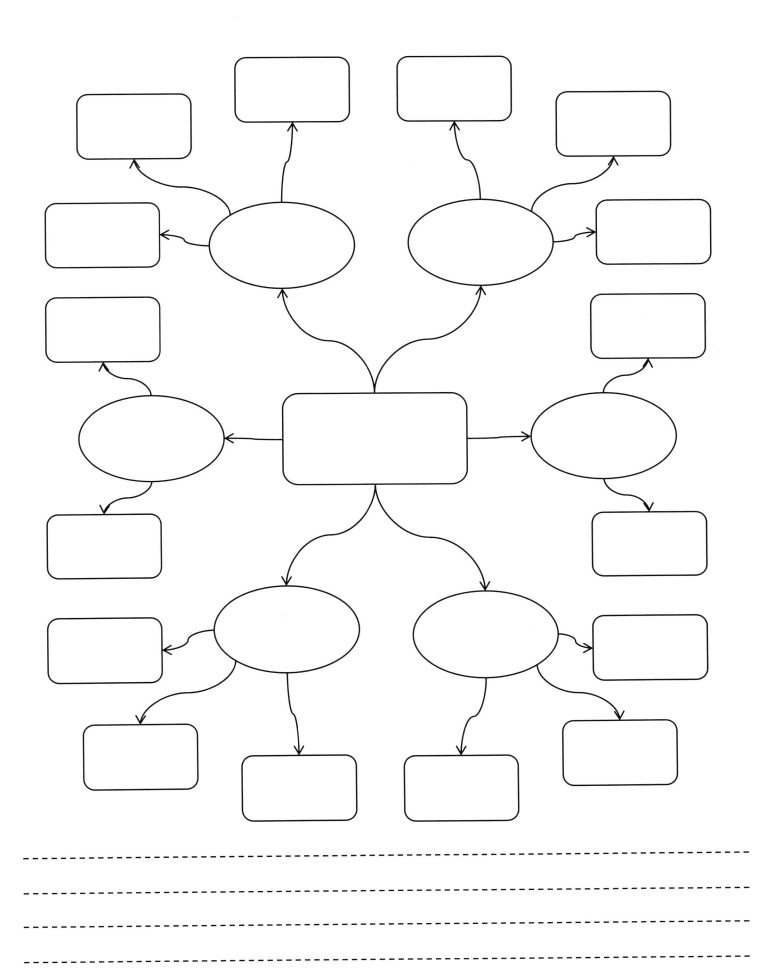

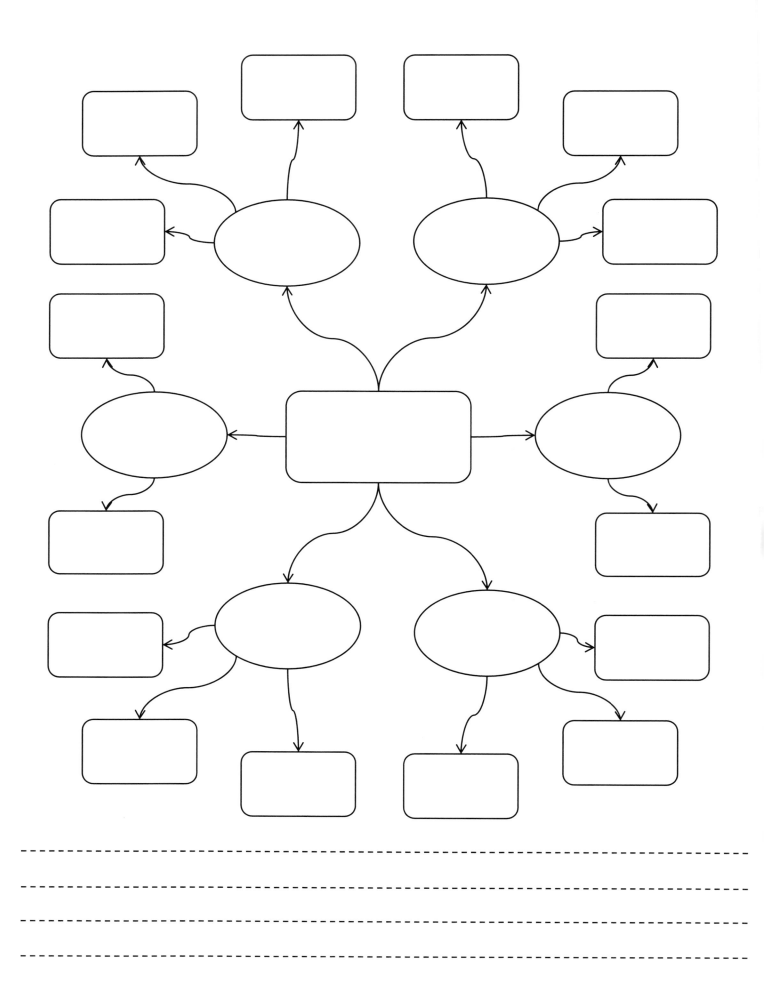

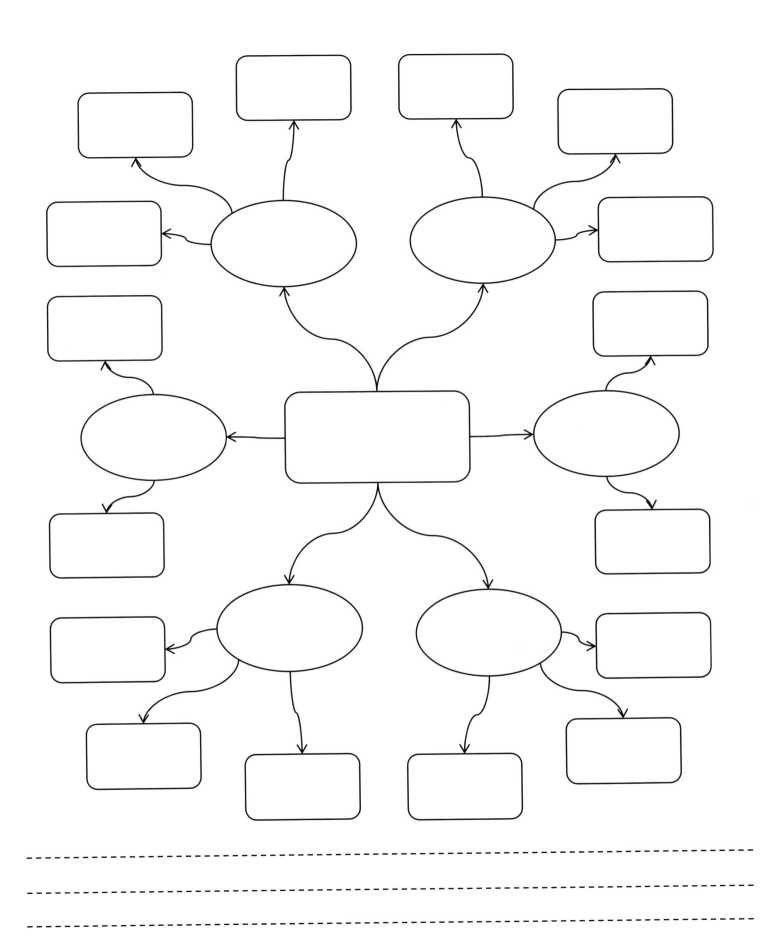

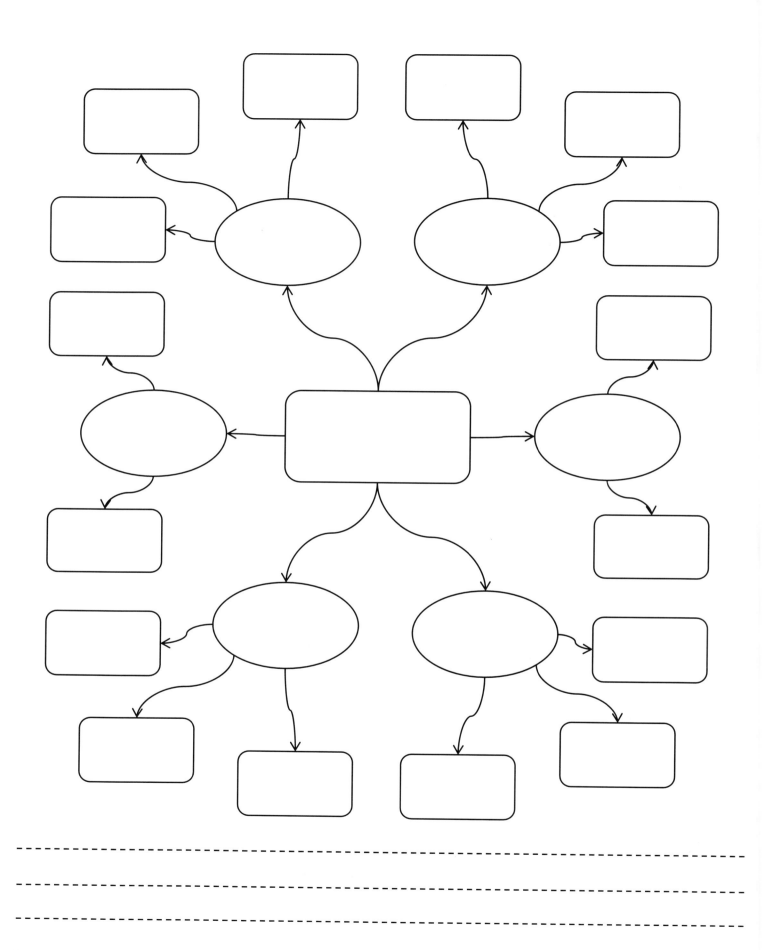

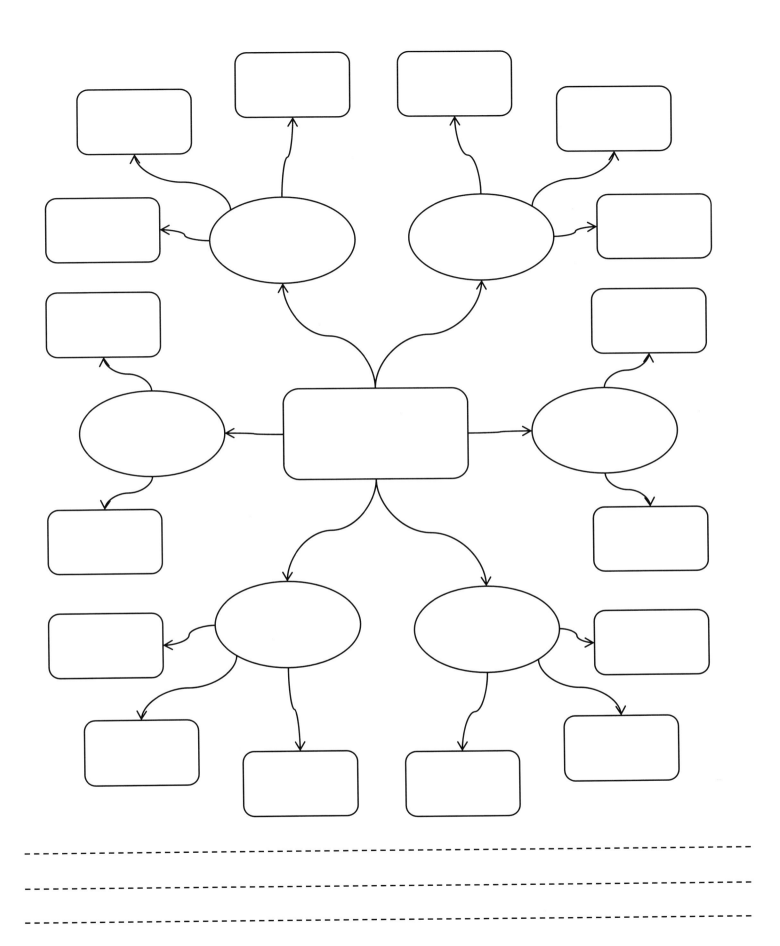

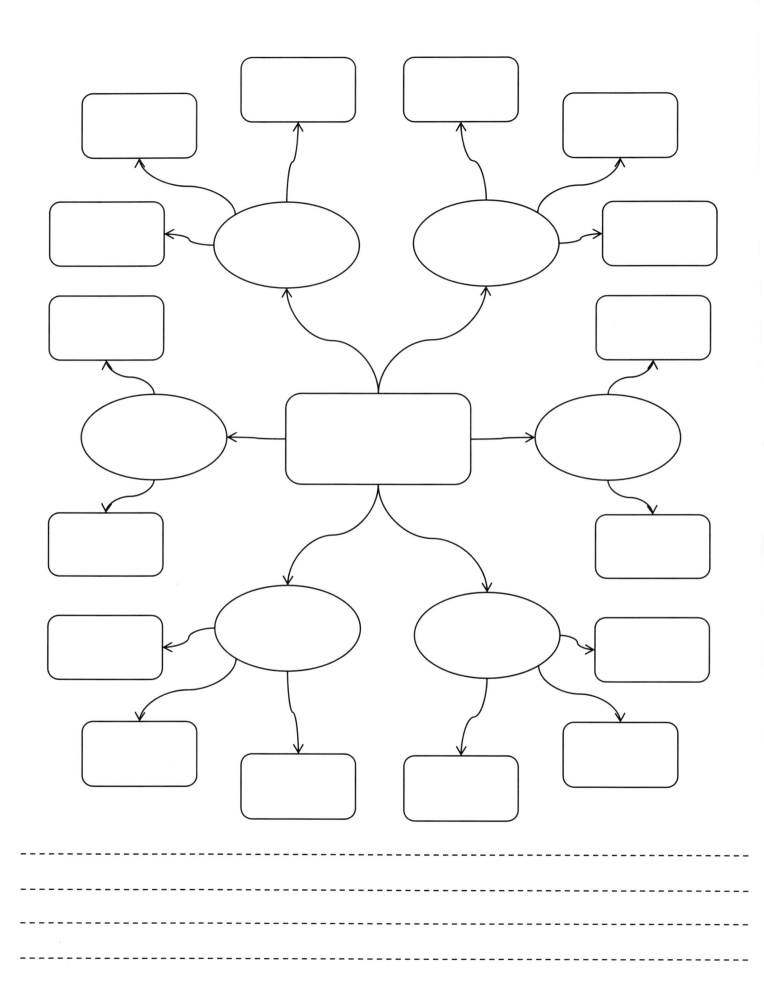

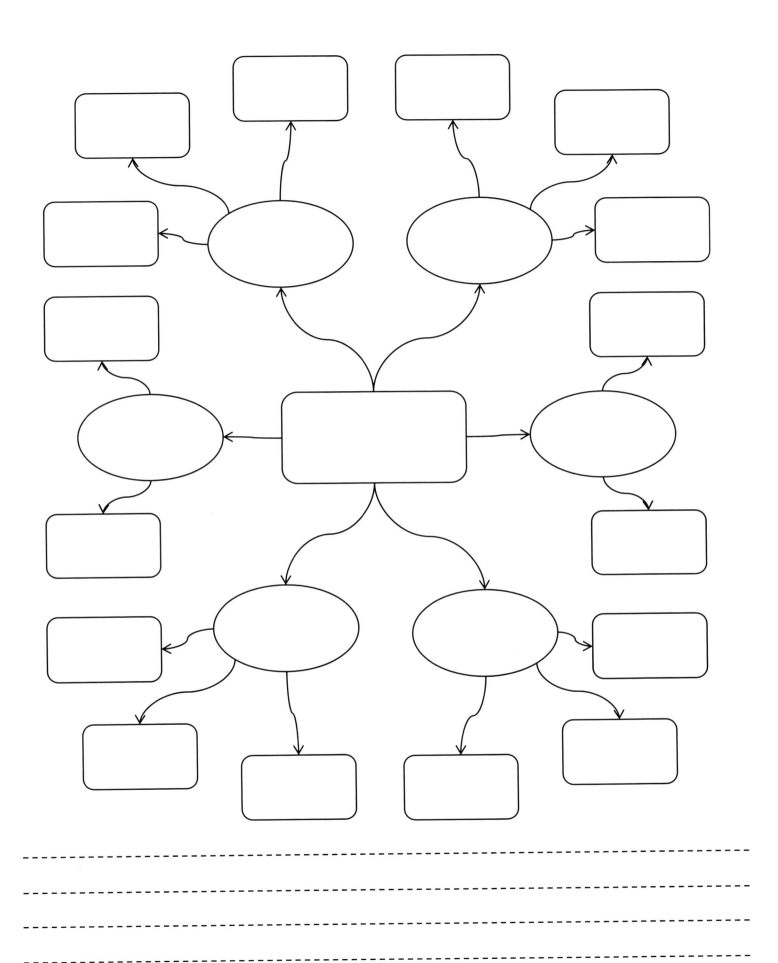

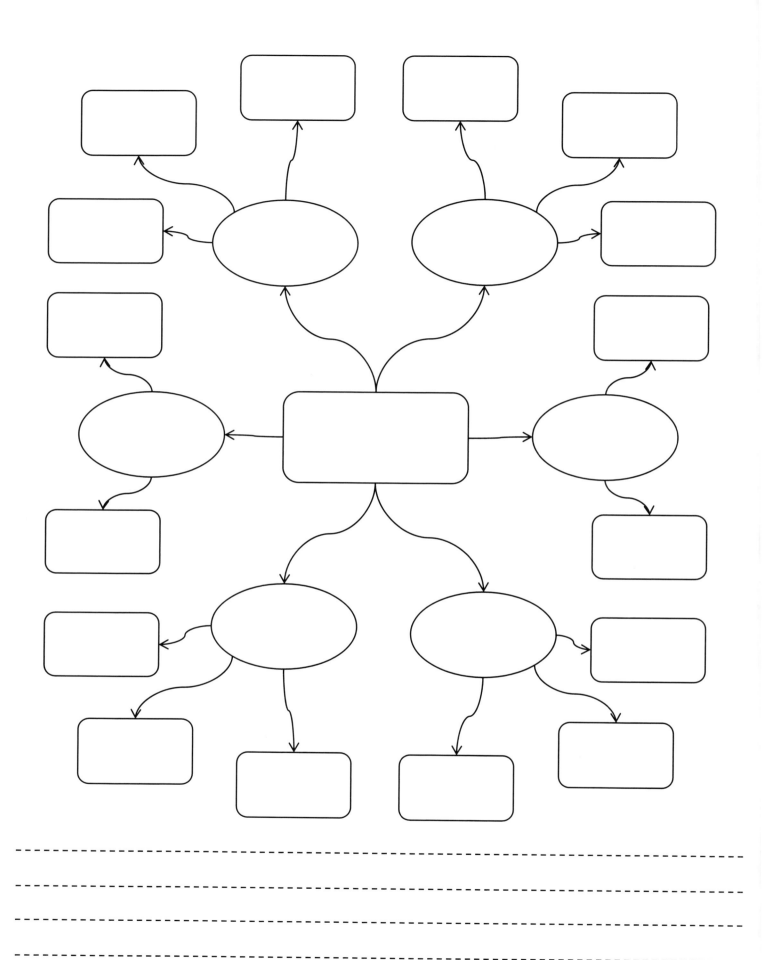

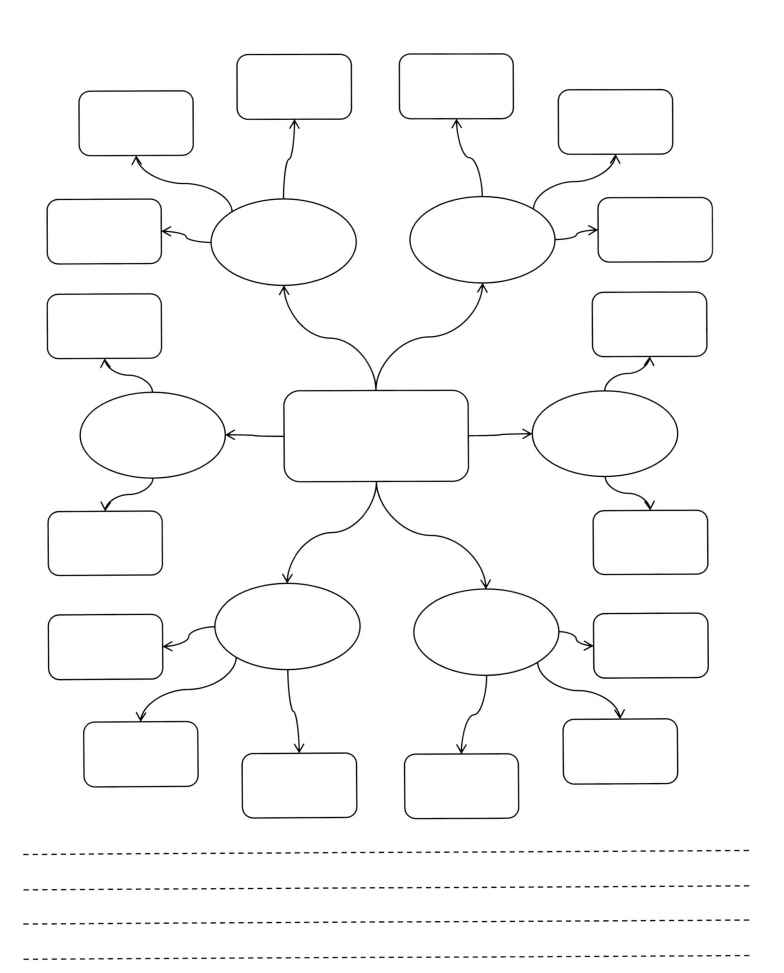

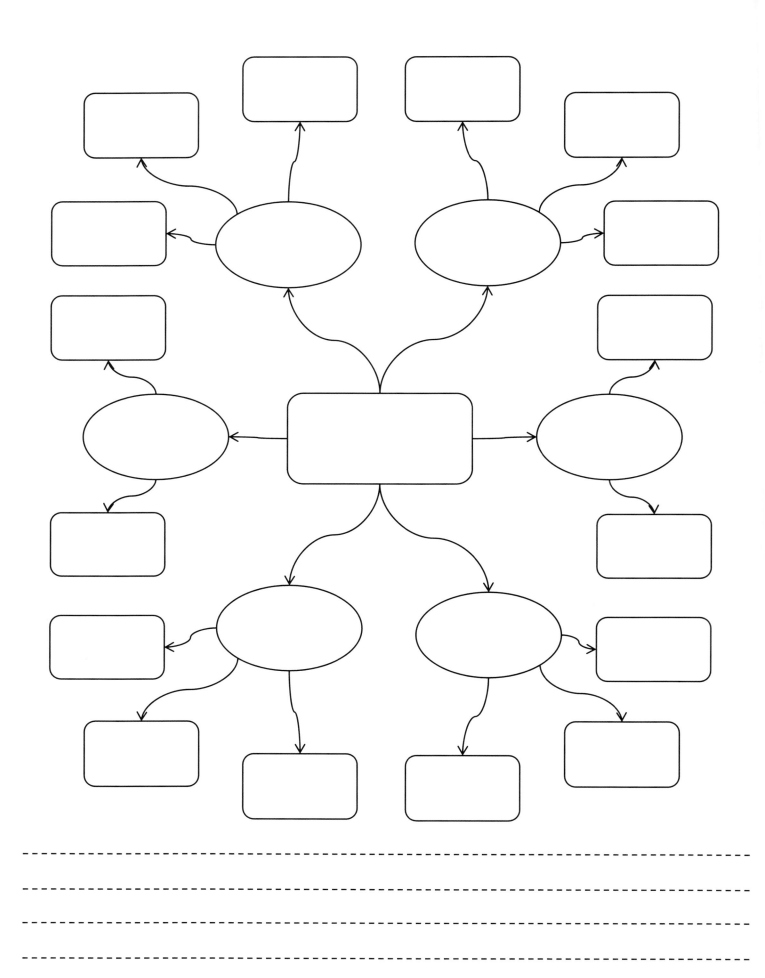

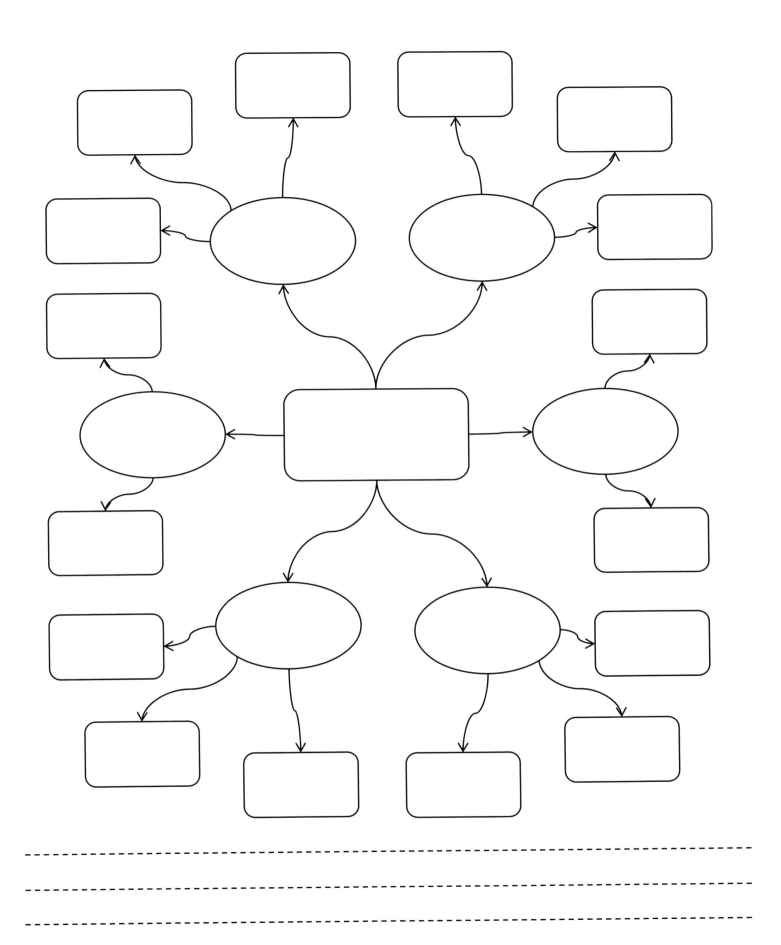

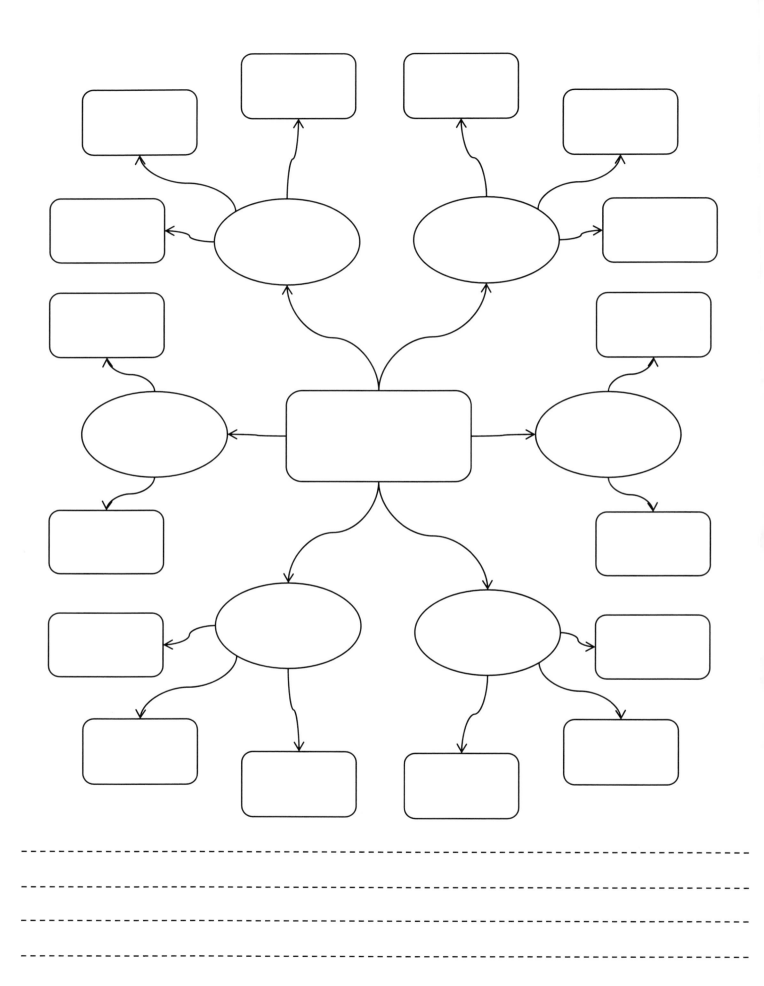

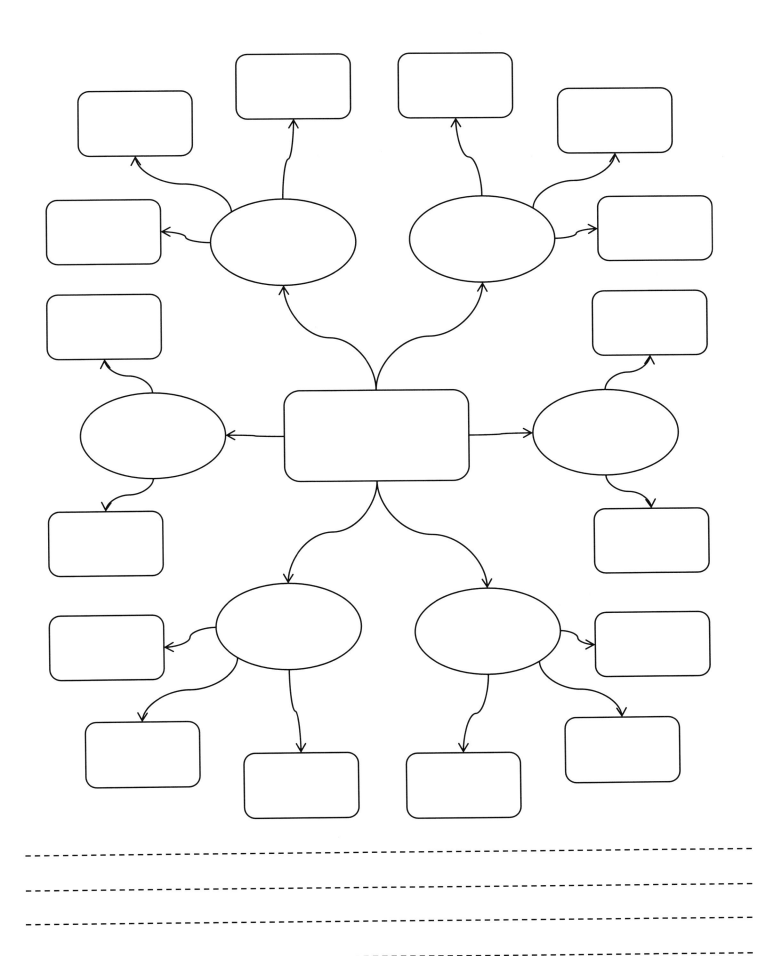

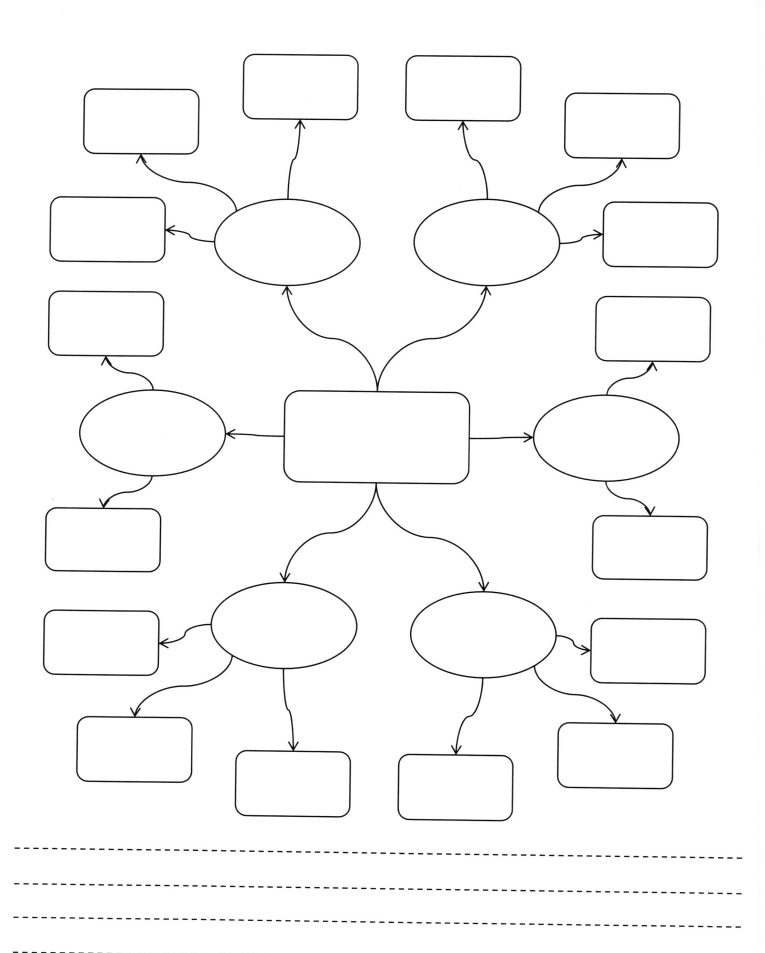

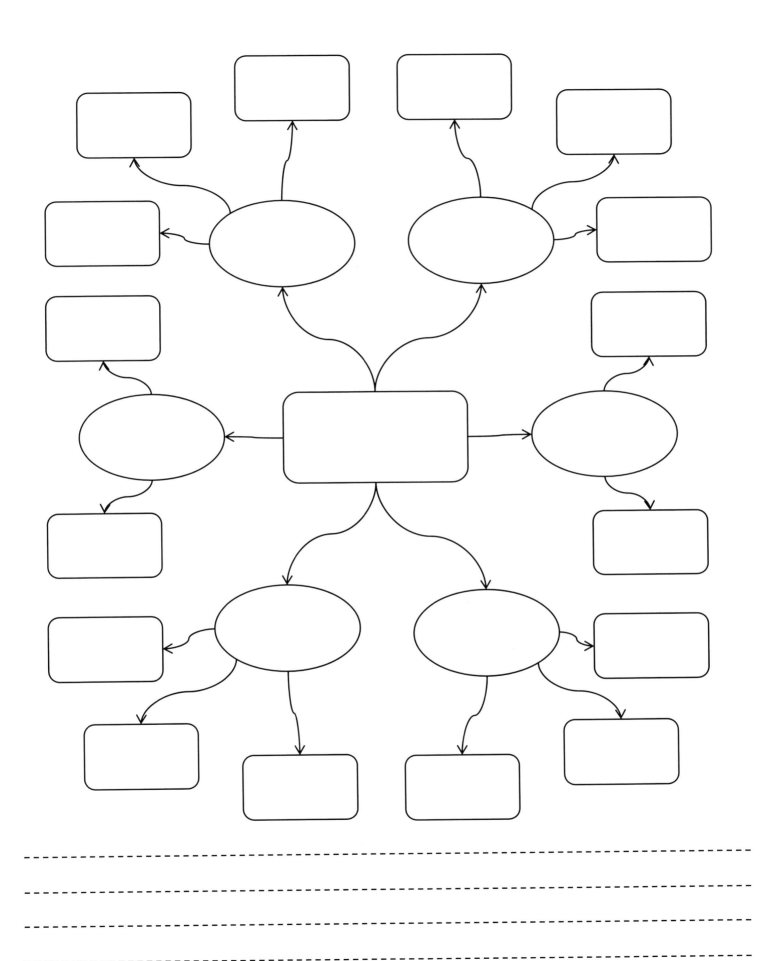

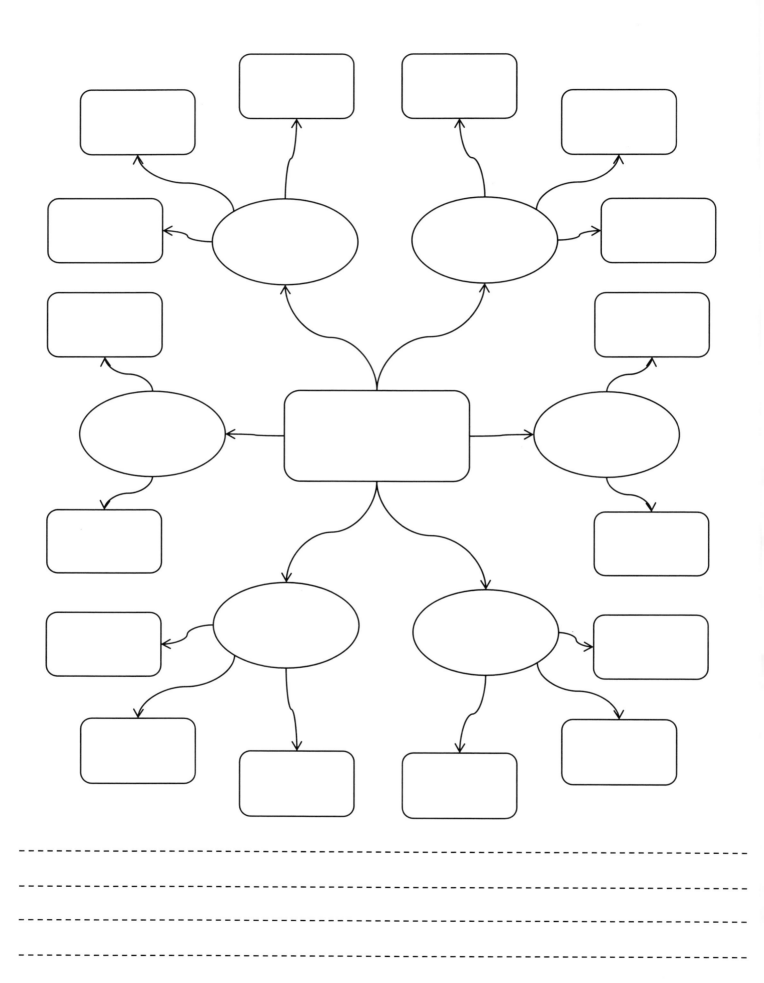

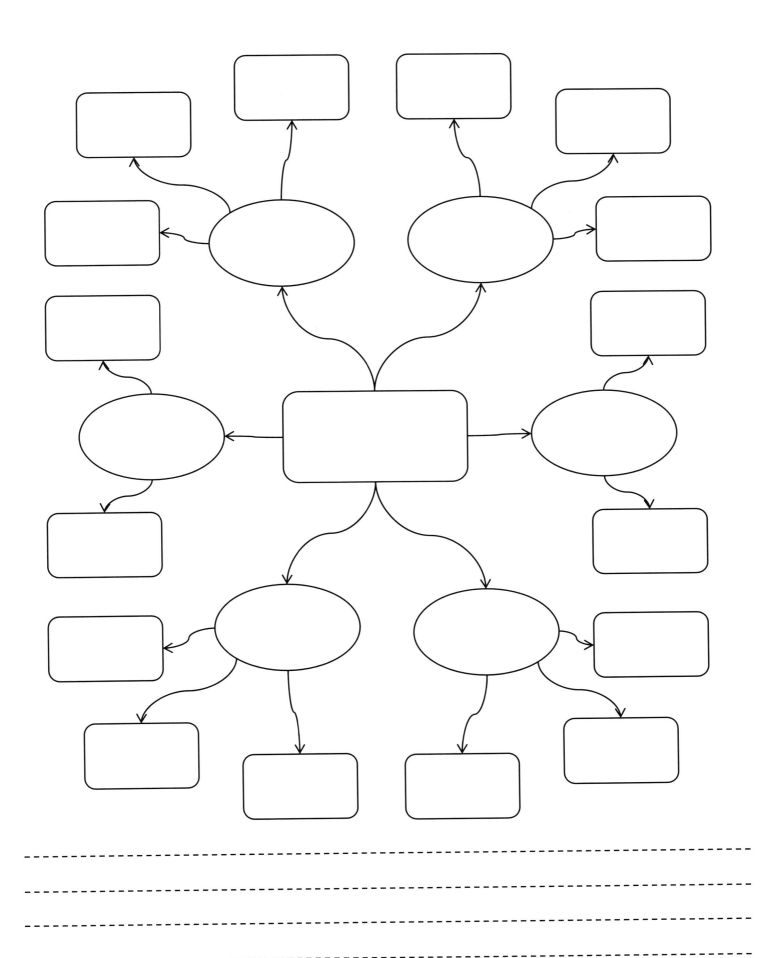

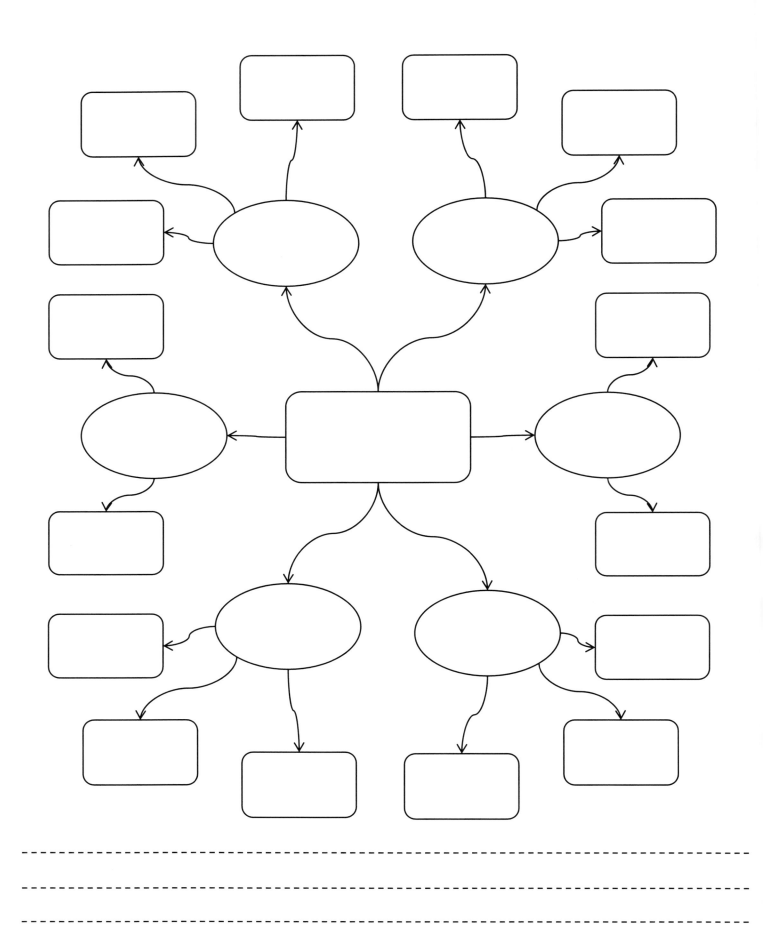

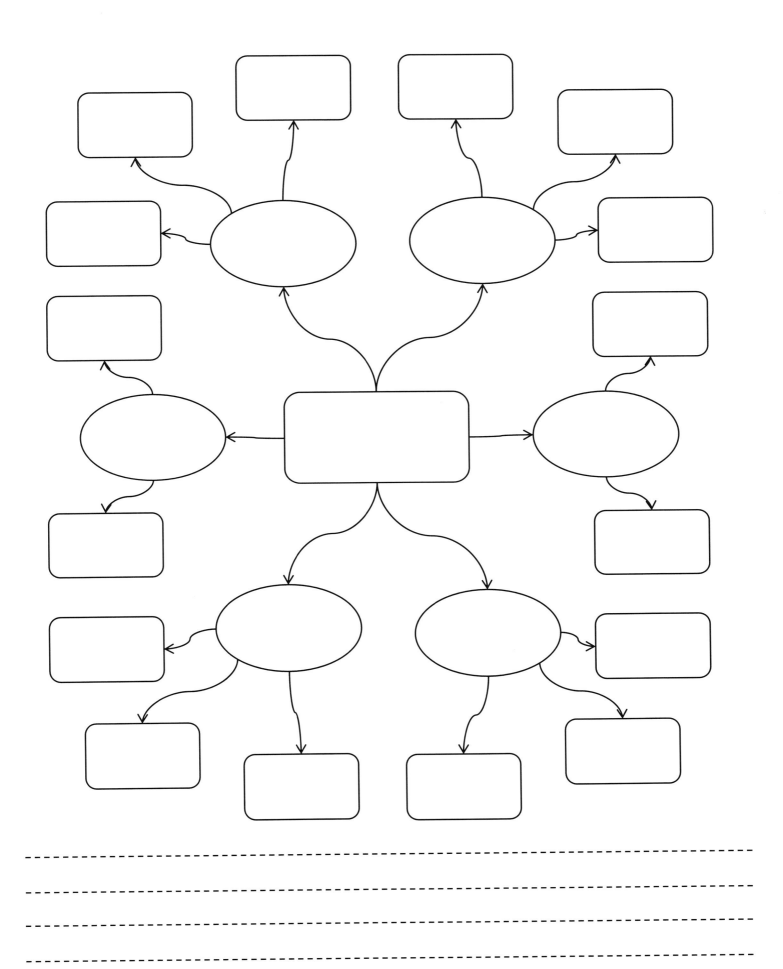

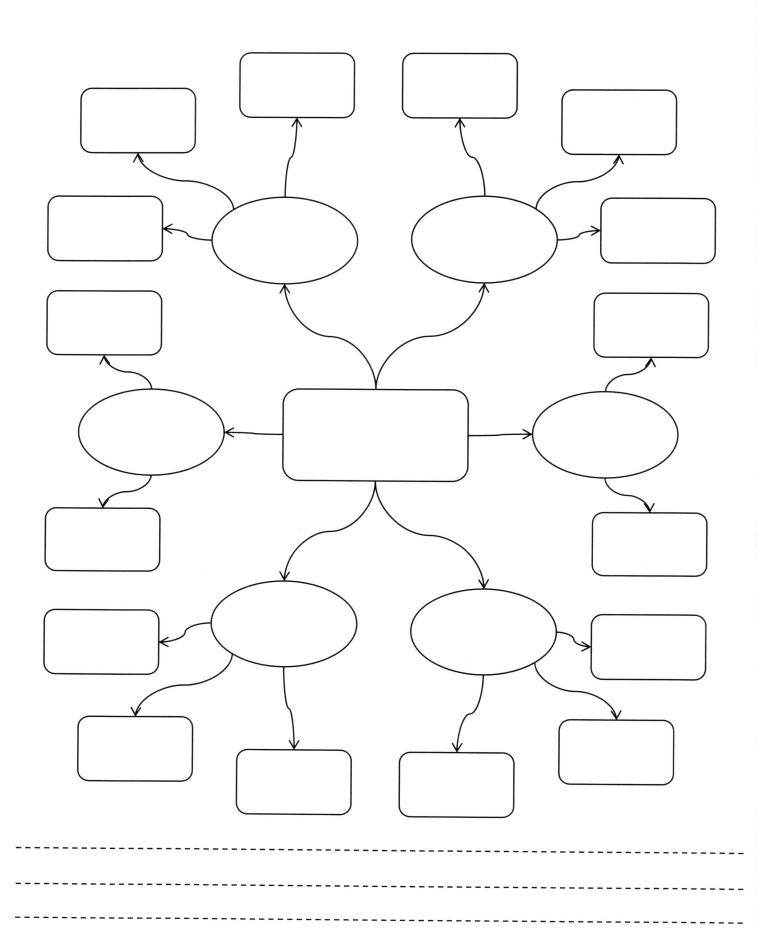

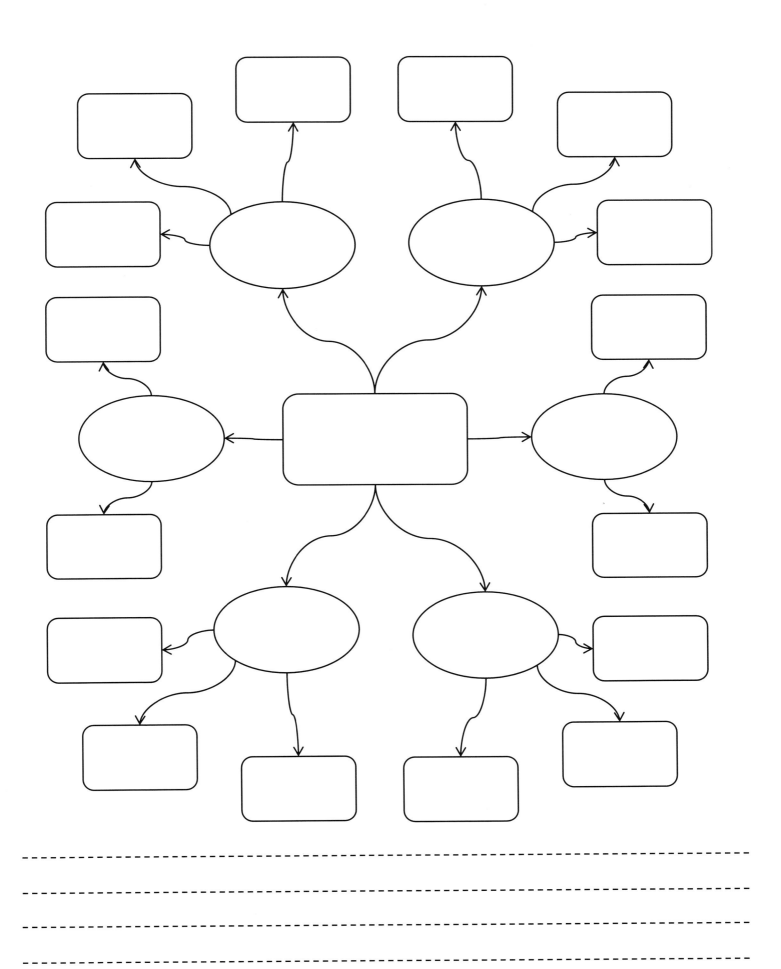

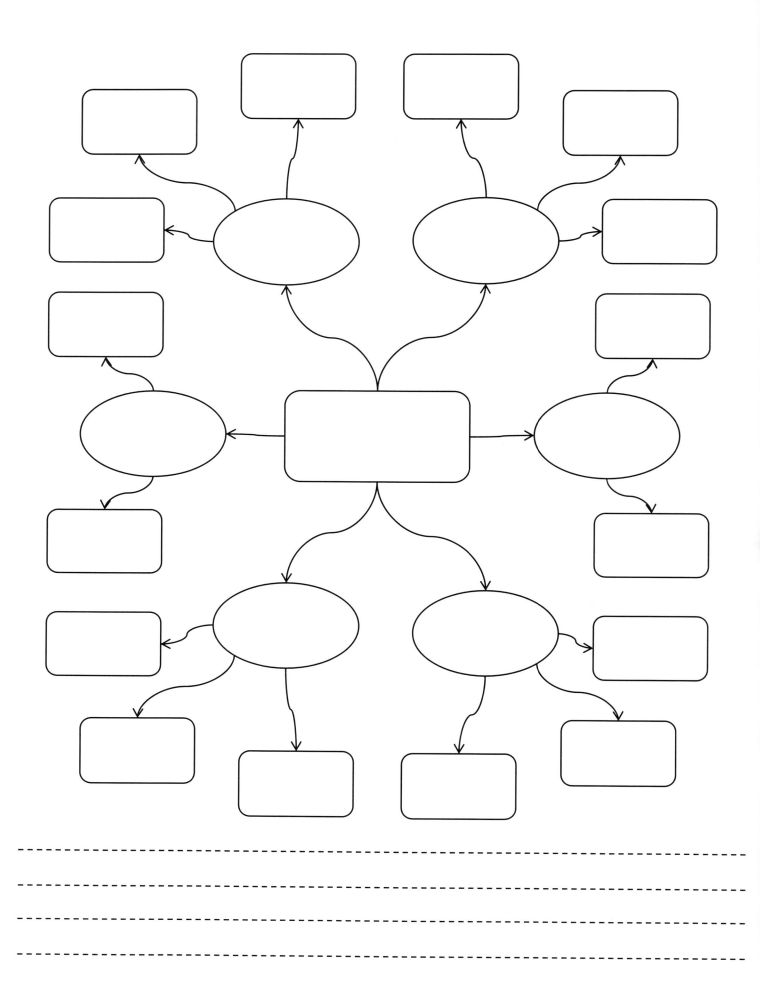

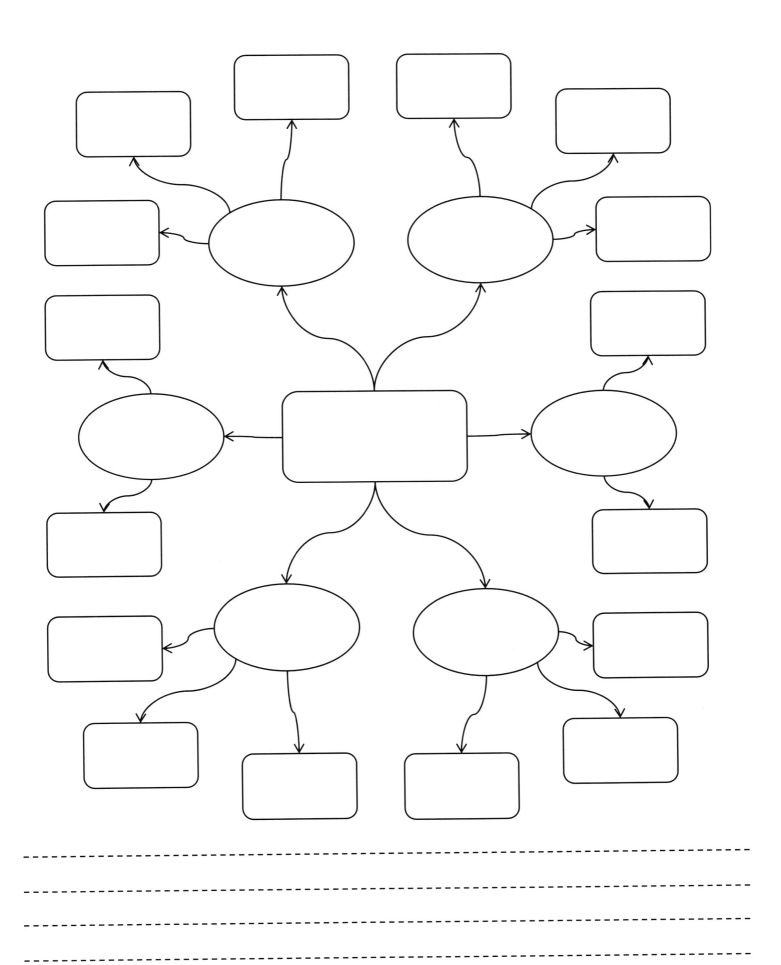

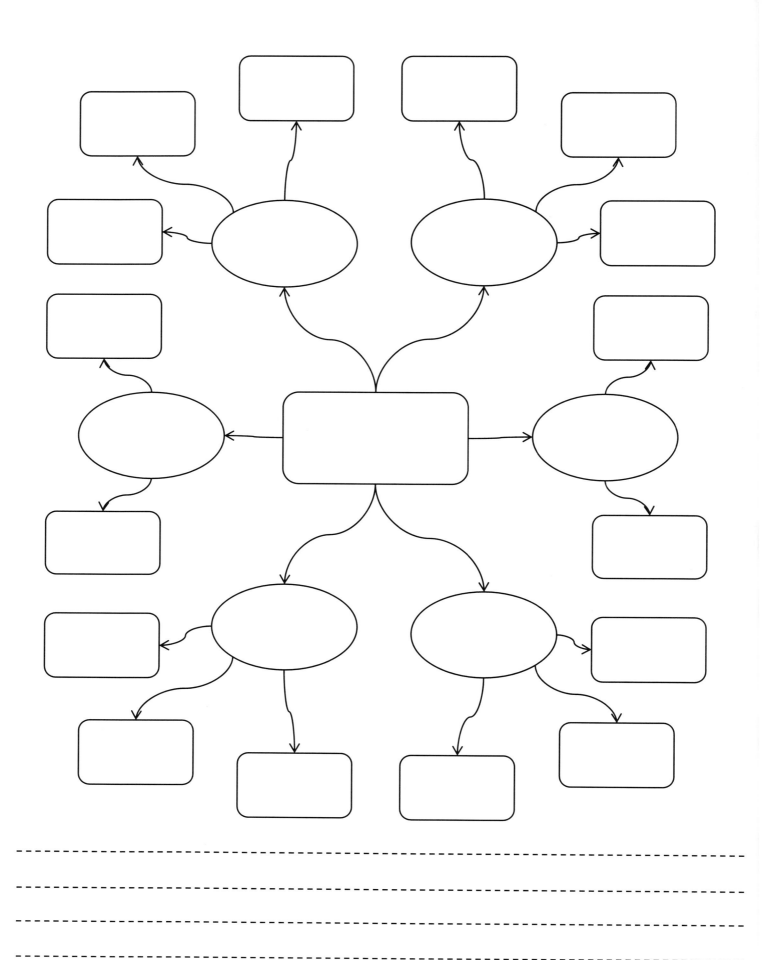

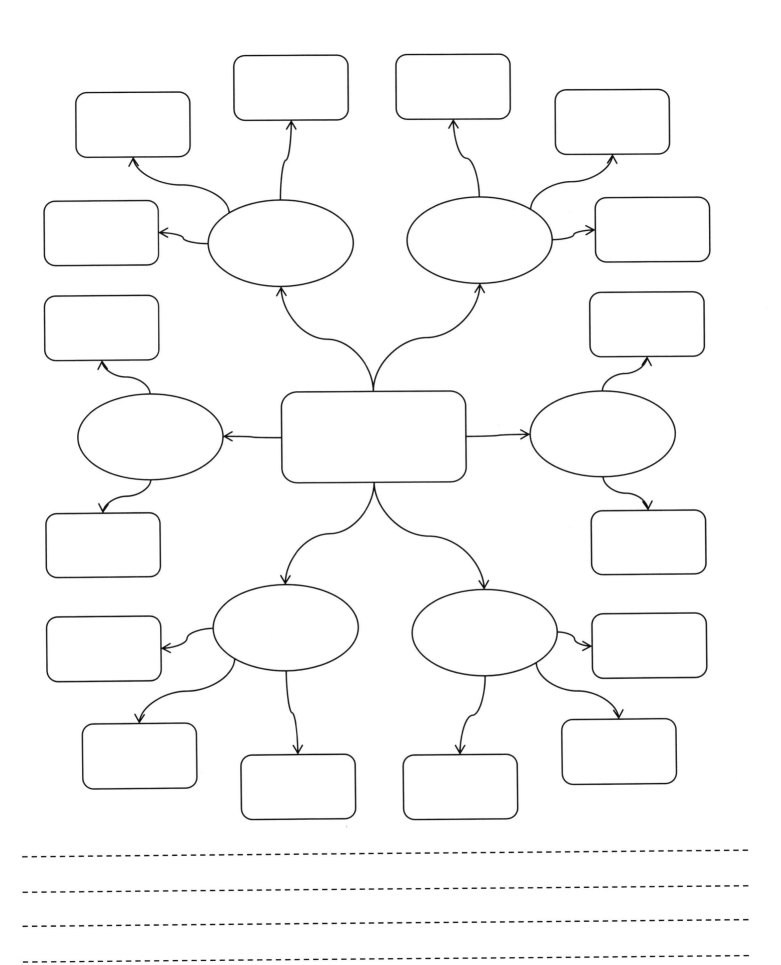

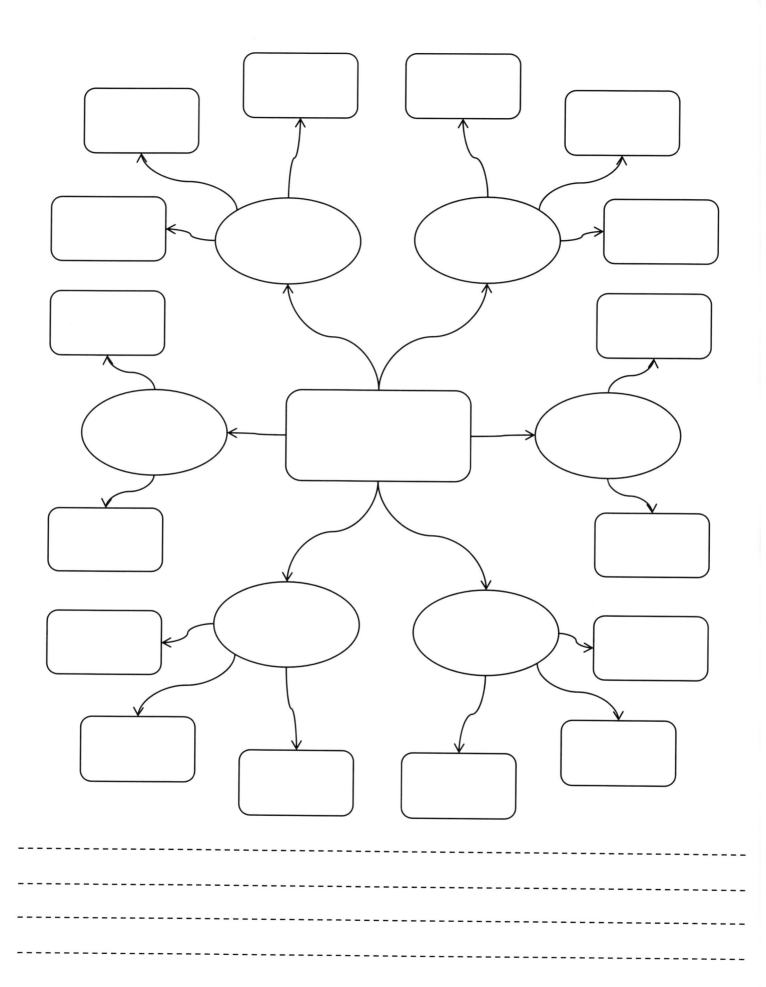

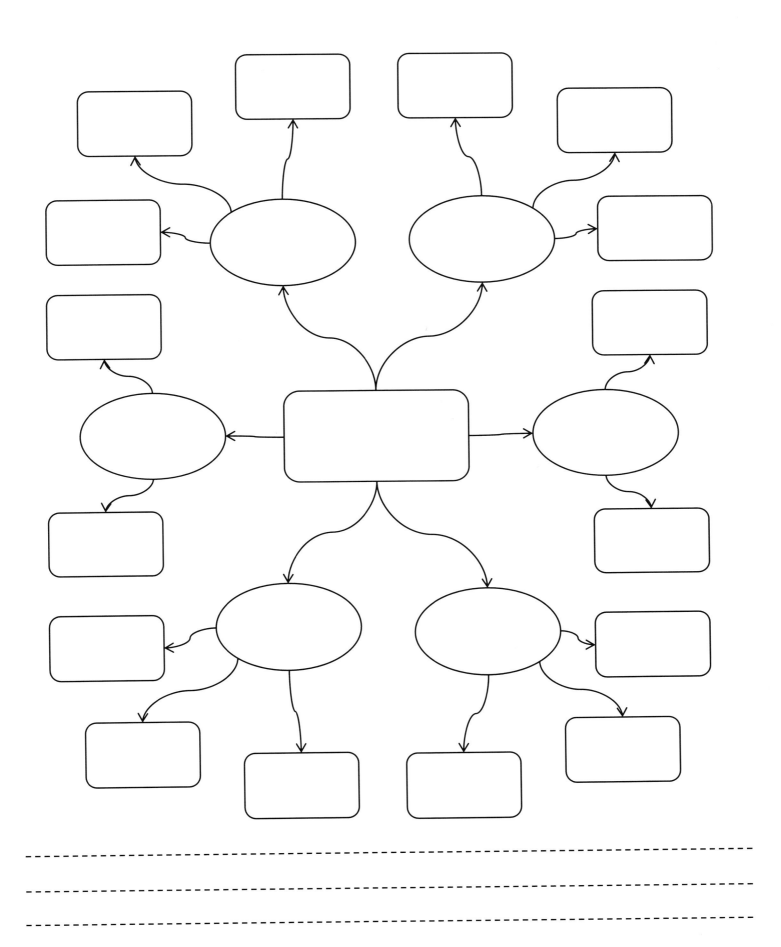

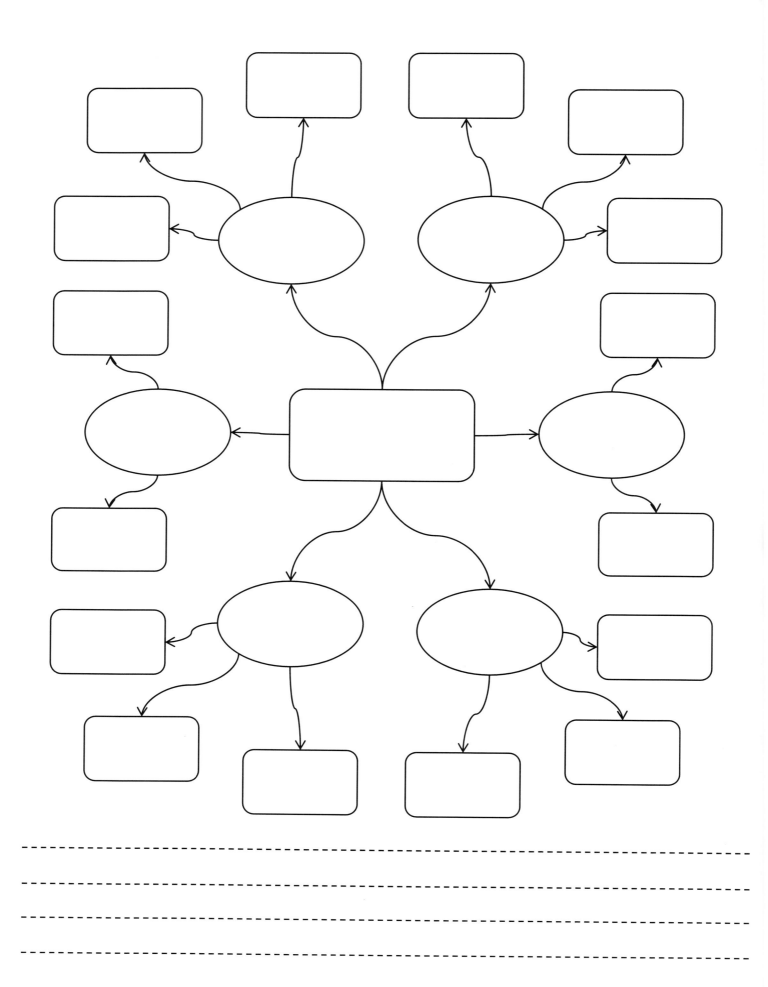

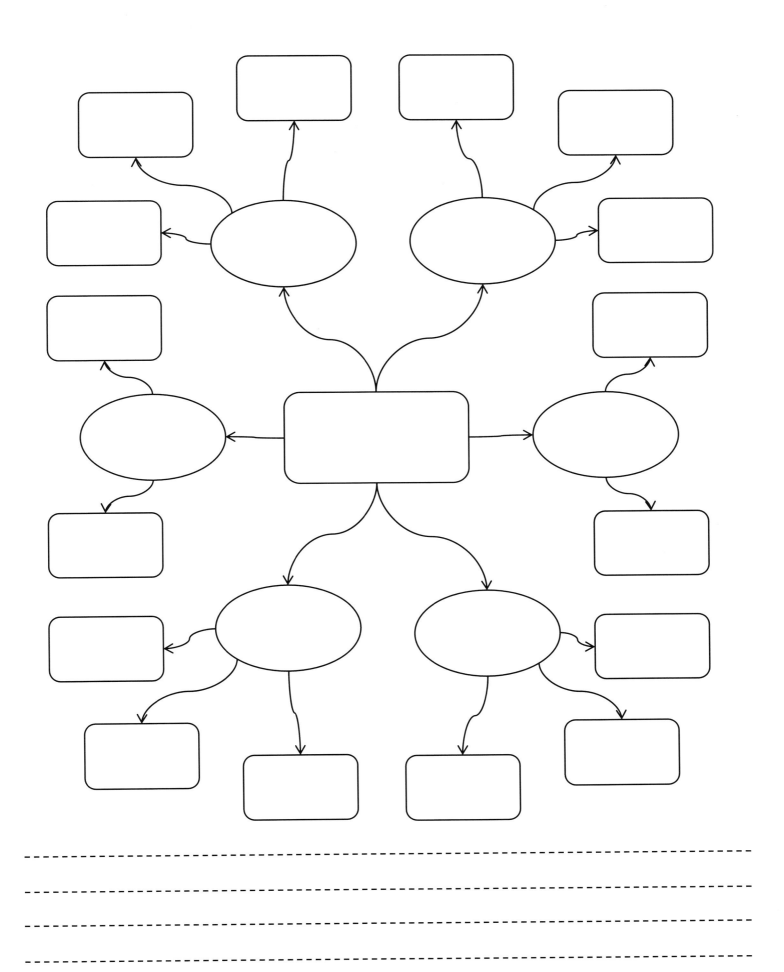

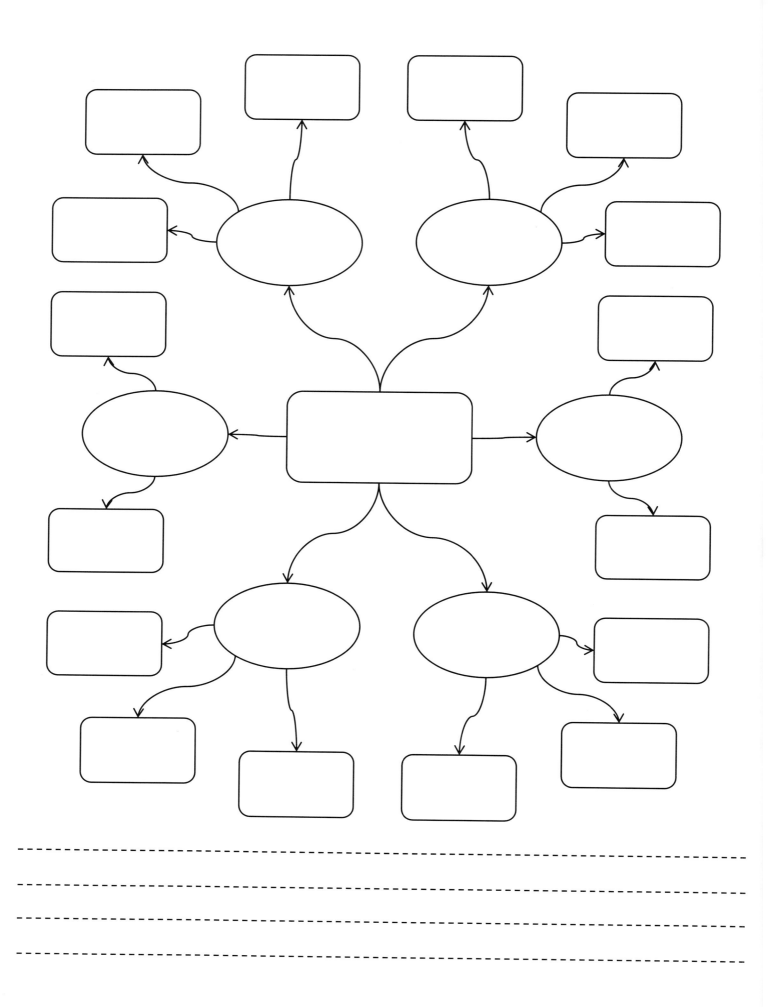

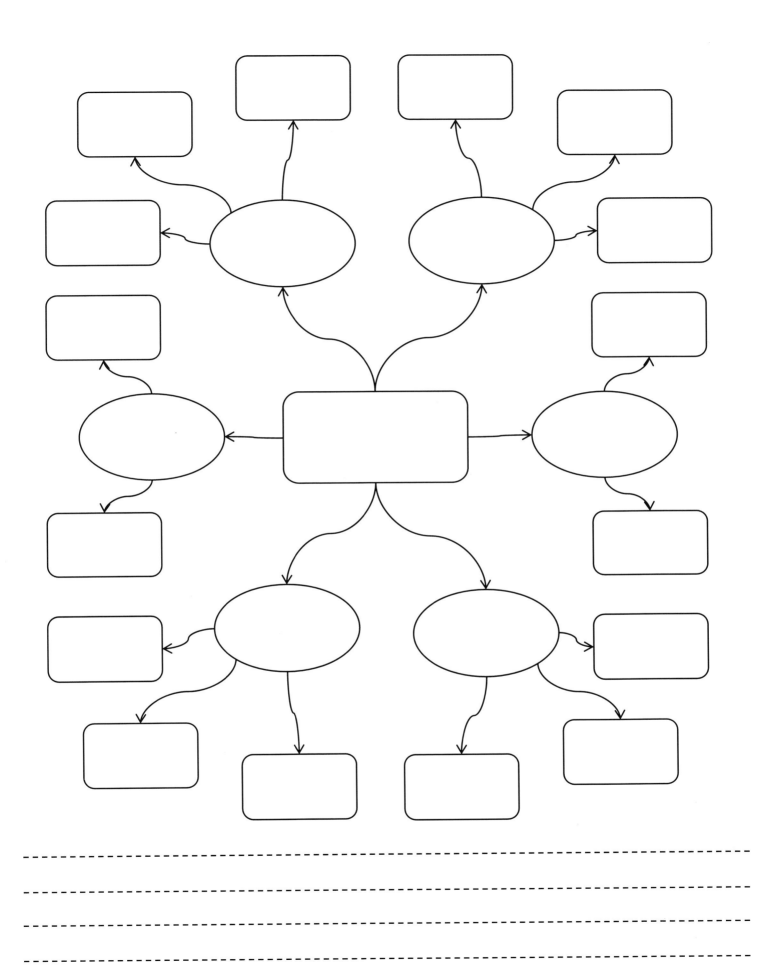

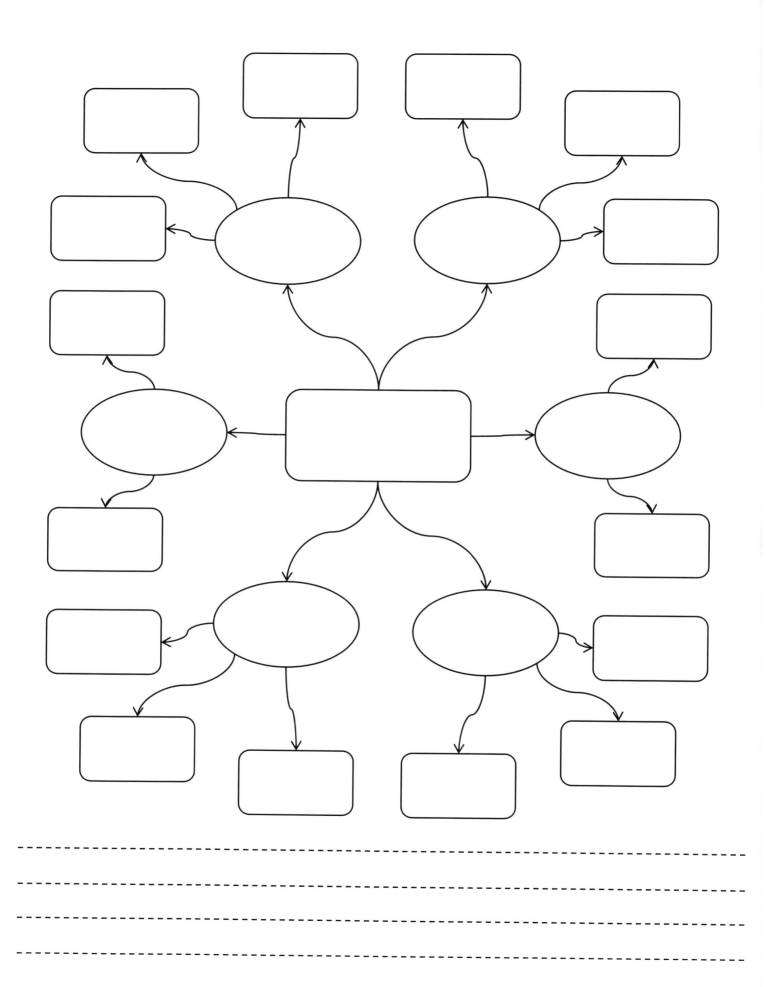

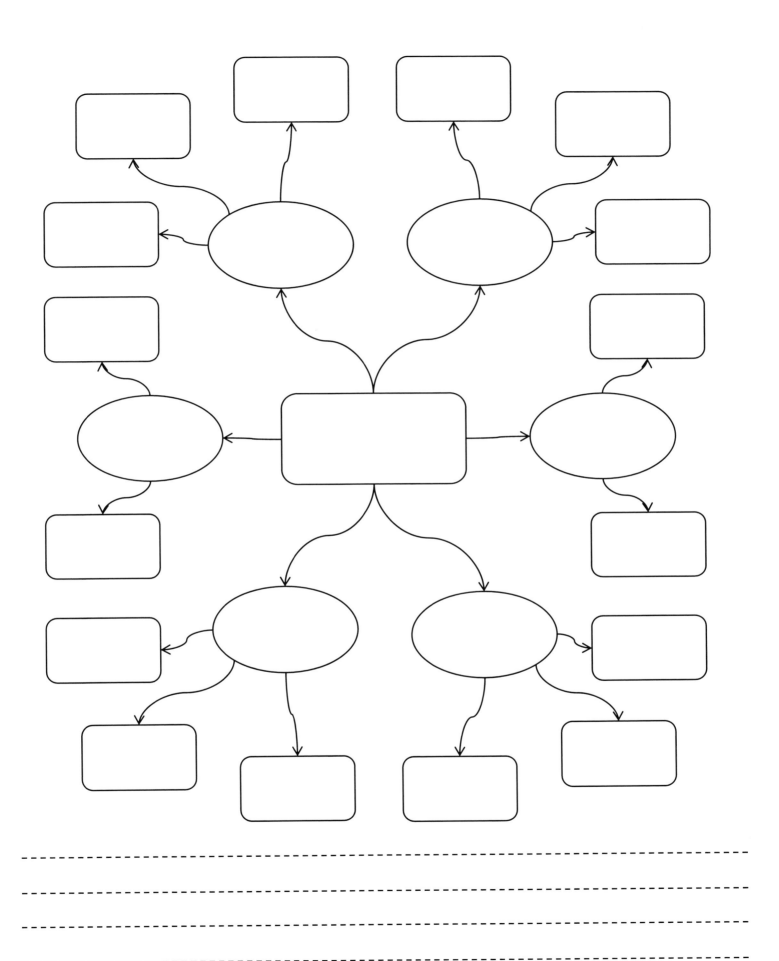

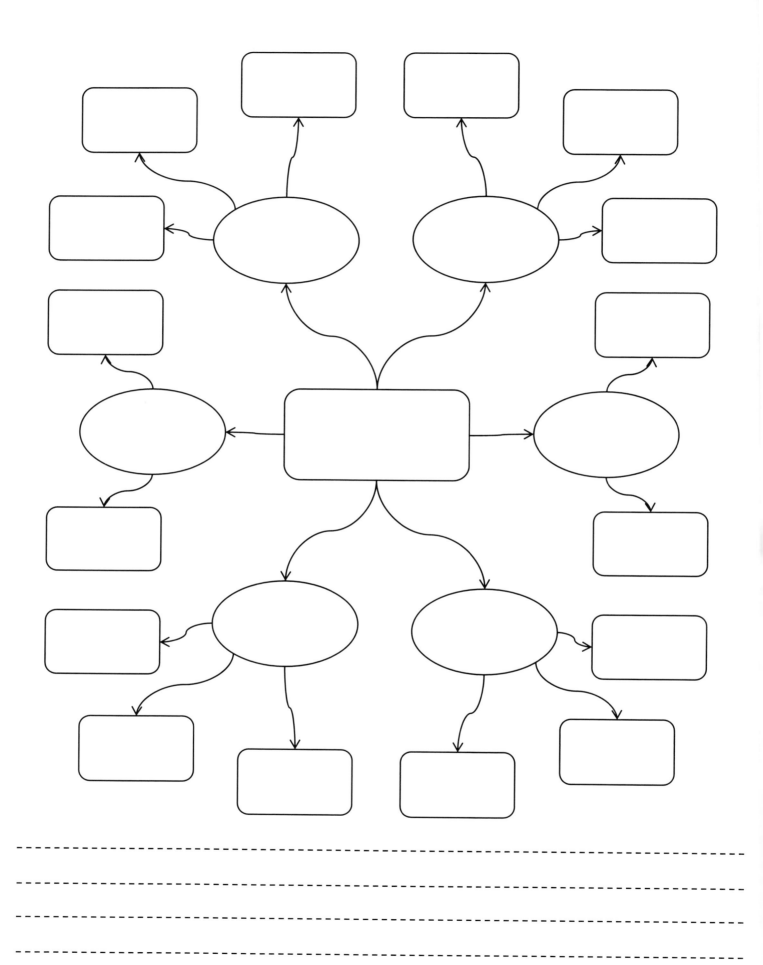

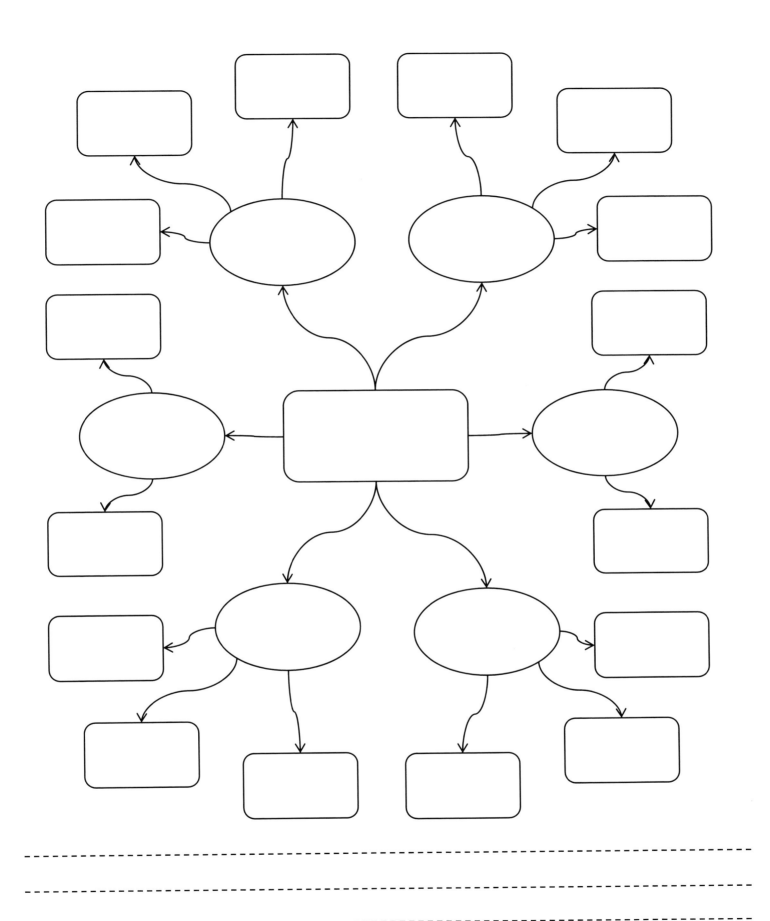

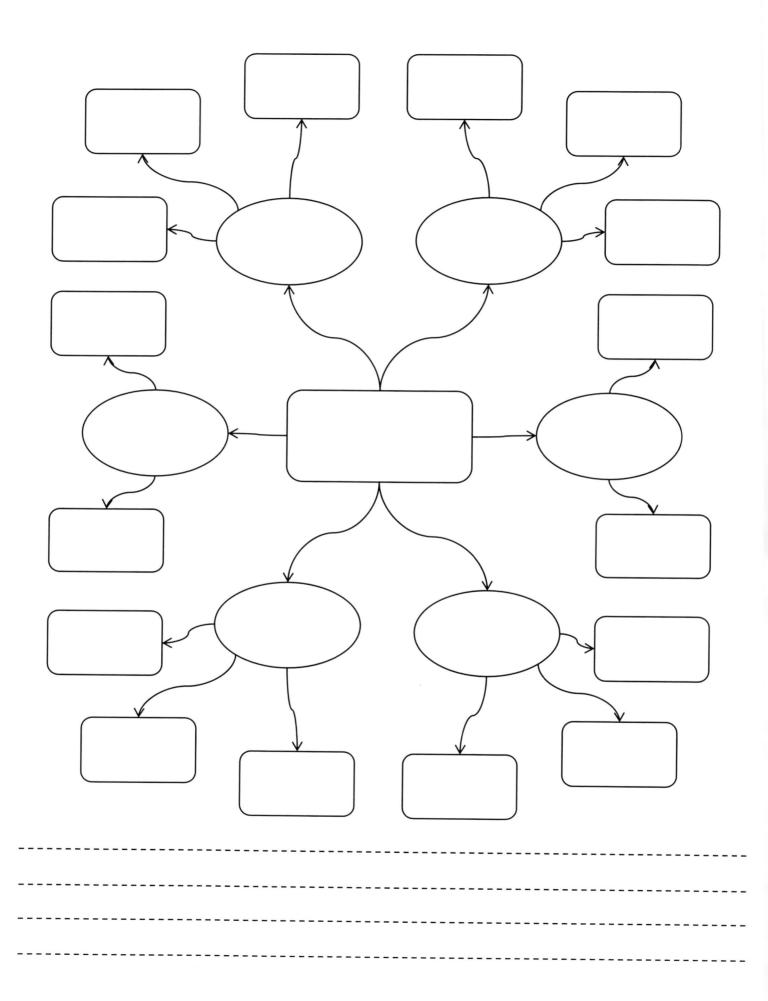

Made in United States
North Haven, CT
02 October 2023

42269648R00061